everything your puppy wants you to know

Also by Louise Glazebrook

The Book Your Dog Wishes You Would Read

LOUISE GLAZEBROOK

everything your puppy wants you to know

S

First published in Great Britain in 2024 by Orion Spring,
an imprint of The Orion Publishing Group Ltd
Carmelite House, 50 Victoria Embankment
London EC4Y 0DZ

An Hachette UK Company

1 3 5 7 9 10 8 6 4 2

A CIP catalogue record for this book is
available from the British Library.

ISBN (Hardback) 978 1 3987 2156 2
ISBN (eBook) 978 1 3987 2157 9
ISBN (Audio) 978 1 3987 2158 6

Typeset by Born Group
Printed and bound in Great Britain by Clays Ltd, Elcograf S.p.A.

MIX
Paper | Supporting
responsible forestry
FSC
www.fsc.org   FSC® C104740

www.orionbooks.co.uk

*I dedicate this book to my children and husband,
who for years and years put up with me disrupting their
weekends by spending every Sunday running puppy
classes in east London.*

*And for every puppy I've encountered, played with,
worked with, taught and been a part of their lives,
I'm forever grateful.*

CONTENTS

Introduction

Even though I work with puppies and their owners every week, and have written a bestselling book about dog behaviour, I am asked almost every day for more specific advice on puppies. There is so much conflicting advice out there, from supposedly 'alpha' trainers to opinionated dog owners in the park, to your vet, not to mention dubious training methods that pop up on our social-media feeds. Is it any wonder that people feel more confused than ever when they bring a new puppy home?

It's not uncommon to see someone in the park with a new puppy looking shell-shocked, clearly wondering if they've made a terrible decision. A new puppy is a chubby delight but also a time-sucking whirlwind: biting fingers, crying, squeezing through gaps you were sure you'd blocked up, weeing everywhere, chewing electrical cables, waking up in the night and wanting your attention all the time.

With millions of puppies entering the world every year, how we breed, raise and train our puppies has never been more important. I want this book to take away your panic and indecision, and help you build your own confidence in understanding your puppy's development and needs. Every puppy is an individual, and your job as its owner is to respect that individuality and work alongside it, rather than try to make it conform to some random timeline when it comes to training goals. Your puppy deserves the best possible start in life, and in this book it's my aim to help you provide that.

Using my years of hands-on experience as a dog behaviourist, and sharing my playful techniques and loving lessons, I'll show you how to make great choices that will set your puppy, and you, up for a wonderful future together.

Inevitably there will be some repetition from my first book, *The Book Your Dog Wishes You Would Read*, because there are some subjects which are too important to leave out of a book on puppies, even if I've written about them before. But my intention is that this is a much deeper dive into the specifics and minutiae of puppy ownership, as that first year – and those first weeks – seem to be the time when so many people struggle.

The other reason I am writing this book is because of a dog called Pudding.

Pudding was an English Bulldog cross who was found on the streets of north London; CCTV showed two men pushing her out of a car and driving away. She was gigantically overweight, with scarring all over her body and missing fur. My parents took Pudding in as a foster, and as a family we rallied around to rehabilitate her, sharing her story on social media.

We learned that Pudding had been used to breed. Forced to have multiple litters, she had been kept contained, not socialised or, as far as we could tell, ever walked. She was so overweight that she had issues with her hips and back legs, affecting her ability to walk, and her own over-breeding meant she was in constant pain. We found she was desperate for human attention, having been starved of it all her short life.

Despite the help of a supportive vet, and all my experience with rehabilitating rescue dogs over many years, after five months my mum and I had to make the painful decision to have Pudding put to sleep. Her behaviour, neurological conditions and medical issues were too much for her body to bear, and too big for this world.

Poor Pudding had been bred badly, raised poorly, unsocialised and unloved. It was devastating to recognise that so much of her suffering could have been avoided if she had been treated differently. It gave us some consolation to know that for her last five months we let her feel grass beneath her feet. She ate freshly cooked food, experienced love and learned to play with a tennis ball. Although she was in considerable pain, on her last day she was sunbathing, being cuddled and I hope she died knowing she was loved. For that, I am grateful that she came to us.

As we took Pudding for her last short walk in a huge field, letting her sniff the scent of deer, I made a promise to myself that I would pass on what I know to stop unsuspecting families bringing home a dog with similar issues.

I've written this book to empower you, to educate and to help you create a brilliant dog with a brilliant future that will be part of your family until death do you part. Dogs are the most incredible creatures and, with the proper care and attention in puppyhood, we can develop a wonderful relationship with them that, if we are lucky, will endure for many years.

Understanding your dog's needs as a puppy is the best thing you can do for your dog's future. If you find this book useful, I urge you to spread the word, so that together we can educate the world and create a better place for us all to live with our dogs. Because for me and, I hope, for you, Dogs Rule.

L
X

CHAPTER ONE

Before You Bring Your Puppy Home

A puppy is one of life's most precious creatures, and raising one is also one of the hardest tasks you will take on as an individual, a couple or a family. You are raising a baby animal that does not speak your language and does not communicate in human ways. Many of the things your new puppy does will make absolutely no sense to you whatsoever (at first). It will feel like you are trying to communicate with an alien, and if you bear that in mind it will allow you to cut yourself and the puppy some slack.

The movies often sell having a puppy as a heartwarming period of fun and laughter. They show the kids laughing while the puppy licks them, or the adult owner enjoying an ice cream in the sun with their new addition sitting adorably at their side. You will definitely get the joyful experiences, but you should also be expecting huge chunks of time and brain power dedicated to believing you are failing, believing you can't do it, thinking you may have made the worst mistake and wondering what on earth has happened to your house, your life and your bank balance. Let me reassure you that this is 'normal'.

This example email from a prospective client sums it up:

Hi Louise,

I don't know what on earth I'm doing with my puppy, I feel swamped. I need help with everything.

Thanks
R

For me, preparation is key, so the biggest thing to really sit and evaluate is: do you have time, right now, to be taking on a puppy and fulfilling its needs?

In order for me to help you make that decision, here are some things that you need to know about taking a puppy on. Realistic expectations will prevent both your heartache and a puppy's life being destroyed because you made the wrong decision.

All relationships need honesty, and taking an honest look at your reasons for getting a dog, your ability to look after one and your capabilities is the kindest thing you can do for yourself and your puppy.

ARE YOU READY TO TAKE ON A PUPPY?

Take the time to consider the following needs of a puppy and ask yourself if this fits into your current life.

- An eight-week-old puppy needs to go out to the toilet every fifteen to twenty minutes. When thinking about working from home, you need to factor in that you will be getting up from your seat every fifteen minutes to take your puppy outside.

- To teach a puppy to feel safe, secure and able to be left at home alone takes months, not days. You won't just be 'popping to the shops' or doing a gym session first thing any more, unless someone else is at home to stay with the pup. You need to factor in that teaching a puppy independence can take six months, at an absolute minimum.

- The days of letting a puppy cry it out at night are, thankfully, over. You will need to either sleep on the sofa with the puppy in the same room, or have the puppy in your bedroom with you, factoring in one to four wake-up toilet breaks, every night, for weeks – until your puppy has learned the bladder and bowel control that only comes with age.

- Your puppy will bite and chew people, and their teeth are needle-sharp. Biting and teething is a developmental period that every single puppy goes through, and there is no way around it. You cannot avoid it, stop it or believe that just because your child doesn't like being bitten your puppy will understand that. Puppies must go through this phase because their teeth are growing, and they are learning about the world.

- You will need to expect eighteen months to four years of work to raise your puppy into a 'dog'. This time varies from breed to breed, as some bigger breeds can develop later and take longer to mature. Please get rid of the notion that within a few weeks you'll have a puppy neatly slotted into your existing routine. Your routine is going to change, for good, and you should see this as a positive!

- Do factor in the kind of cost your puppy may bring to your life. To give you some examples of how much my dog Pip costs me per month (he is over ten years old at the time of writing):
  - » Pet insurance is £90 per month.
  - » Dog walker for two walks per week is £18 per walk – £144 per month.
  - » Raw food is £160 per month (he weighs 29 kilos).
  - » Treats and chews are at least £30 per month.
  - » Medication for his arthritis is £100 per month.
- Who will look after your puppy when you go away for work or on holiday? I've found so many people don't consider this, let alone discuss it, before getting a puppy. Most people who are employed will get four to six weeks of annual leave. So, if you were planning for your dog to be with your dog walker during those weeks you are away, you could estimate that at £35–50 per day, so six weeks of holiday dog care would cost you £1,470–£2,100 as a minimum.

I have no wish to suck the joy out of your decision to get a lovely cuddly puppy, but these essential considerations are a stark reminder of what you are taking on. It's crucial to consider them all carefully, and to be informed about the right situation, the right set-up and the right time of your life to be undertaking this epic responsibility.

BRINGING A PUPPY HOME IF YOU ALREADY HAVE A DOG

I often hear clients say that they would like to get another dog, when they have an existing dog at home. And that can be a lovely idea providing you have thought about the right dog to join your family. It is worth pointing out that many dogs would prefer to live out their years as a solo dog, as most would prefer not to share the limelight! If you are thinking of taking on a second dog, you should be thinking about a few things, and below are just some topline thoughts you need to have. This is something I would discuss in great detail with my clients, but to get you started:

- How old is your current dog and what age of new puppy would be the right fit? For example, does your dog not tolerate puppies well in the park? In which case, you would be better to think about getting an older rescue dog you can more easily integrate.
- What is your existing dog's personality? Sadly, this gets overlooked so many times, and it is one of the most critical considerations before you move forward. Some rescues will ask that a puppy is only rehomed with an existing older, very confident and happy dog, because they need that puppy to have a great mentor. The personality of the puppy you choose will deeply impact your dog at home, and it could be the best or worse decision you make.

9

- Do not presume that your dog will just open their home and paws to a new dog coming in. Just yesterday I was at a foster carer's home who had a nine-week-old puppy in her care – this puppy had been taken home that day by a family with an existing dog, but the dog did not accept it and so the family gave the puppy back immediately. This is the reality of what is happening with puppies and rescue dogs. You need to think deeply about how your dog interacts with other dogs in real life . . . Do they actually like their company? Do they play with them or not?

There is much more to think about, but I hope this has made you realise that it isn't just as simple as get two dogs and all will be merry and well!

WHY TAKING TWO WEEKS OFF WORK ISN'T ENOUGH

I'm so sorry to be the bearer of bad news, but it's so important to understand that a puppy needs far more from you than just two weeks off work.

I get emails like this all the time:

We are getting a puppy on Sunday and we have taken the next two weeks off work. In that time, we would like to get our puppy sorted and ready to be left when we return to work.

Dogs don't do things on a timeline that make sense to us. They have their own feelings, personalities, patterns and needs and it's essential to understand that two weeks won't even begin to touch the sides for what your puppy is going to need from you.

Please don't imagine that, after the first two weeks have passed, you will be merrily marching off to your home office to crack on while your puppy snoozes. You can expect to be working late into the night to make up for the work you missed that day, constantly distracted by a teething, tired, energised, rampant, playful, chewy puppy who needs attention, contact and training.

To raise a happy, confident, resilient, well-adjusted puppy, we need to have got them from a great breeder or a reliable rescue. And then we need to provide them with training, stimulation, play, exercise, love and consistency. In my experience, it takes a minimum of eighteen months to start to see the hard work of raising and socialising a puppy pay off. Two weeks would be around 2.5 per cent of that timeline! Your time and efforts will pay off when you have chosen a great dog and put the work in. The dog you will end up living with will be a delight and you will be so grateful for all your efforts and consistency.

In addition to this, I really do not recommend you take two weeks off and then employ a walker or some kind of doggy day care for five days per week. Your puppy is going to go through so many developmental periods, and will have so many needs from you as its owner (reassurance, consistent contact, learning about independence) that you are asking for issues by shipping the puppy off to someone else for such a large part of each week.

If your intention when getting a puppy is to use day care and walkers five days per week, I would strongly urge you to not get one at this time in your life. Instead, set yourself and your dog up for success: get an older rescue dog who doesn't need as much stimulation and exercise and who is happy to snooze the days away – greyhounds are a great option.

Lastly, we need to remember that you are taking on a puppy to be a part of your life and family. For it to be collaborative, that journey starts from the day you bring your puppy home, which is why figuring out your timing is key.

A puppy doesn't know or care if you have a big project coming up, your boss is in town or you need to work fourteen-hour days out of the house. If you are choosing to bring a puppy into your home, it is your responsibility to think about all of your current and future work demands. Either you will have to adapt your work to find a time that will work for you and your puppy, so that you can give them what they need and you can enjoy it, or accept that this isn't the right time. Taking on a puppy when you don't have the time or the attention to give to it isn't fair on the puppy, and it isn't fair on you either.

You may also end up with bigger issues to resolve if you don't put the proper time into doing things well. Separation anxiety is so easily created with a puppy, by forcing them to be left while you go to work having done no consistent, week-by-week preparation. By not putting the work in early doors, you will end up paying for it both financially, behaviourally and emotionally as small issues get bigger, then take longer to work on, over more time, which costs more money as you are more likely to need a dog behaviourist like me in your life to help you.

My motto with all dogs and puppies is 'set them up to succeed'. It's so much easier to establish good habits than it is to manage issues that have been created over time. A mere two weeks at home with your puppy will not set them up for success. You will feel rushed, worried and frustrated because your puppy isn't 'getting it' as quickly as you want them to. Our puppies and dogs mirror our emotions, we cannot deny this, and that means an anxious, confused and frustrated puppy, which won't be what you had hoped for.

WHY THE BREED YOU CHOOSE IMPACTS EVERYTHING

Every puppy has their own distinct personality which evolves from many factors, such as how they were bred, how and where they were raised, what food they were fed and so much more. Some of this you can control, some of it you can't. But one thing that we as humans have a huge amount of control over is the breed we decide to bring home. Plus the personality and temperament of the dog that we select.

I have written about this in a lot of detail in *The Book Your Dog Wishes You Would Read*, but as breed selection is so crucial some of it bears repeating here.

As part of my one-to-one consultancy work, I help people make an informed decision about which breed fits with their needs. We work closely together to determine what it is that they want from a dog and how we can match that up and select a breed that will thrive with them. As a society, we tend to make snap decisions based on how a dog looks. I agree that there needs to be a physical appeal but if that is your main deciding factor, you are very likely to take on a dog that isn't right for you and one which could actively make your life miserable. Not to mention the dog's life being downright depressing because they are not being given what they need to thrive.

Here are the top five dogs that I find people are physically drawn to but with no understanding of the needs of the breed. In no particular order:

- The French Bulldog – people think they are cute and love the 'colours' that they come in without realising that, if they are over-bred, their flat faces can cause them huge breathing problems. Some breeders are breeding only for colour, rather than behaviour and health, creating blue, lilac and cream dogs – but inbreeding can cause health problems. These colours are not the standard colours for this breed, and that can create issues. We also have to look at the ethics of breeding a dog that struggles to breathe properly when, by simply elongating their snout, we could solve many health issues for this breed.
- The Hungarian Vizsla – loved because they are sleek, long eared and ginger – yet they are also one of the most sensitive breeds I work with that need a huge amount of owner input, and isn't the best choice for most people, especially not first-time dog owners.

They are a working breed designed to do a job that requires a great deal of energy.

- The Blue Staffordshire Bull Terrier – often bought because it is 'blue' without understanding of what breeding specifically for that colour gene can create within a breed. Blue Staffies are one of the breeds I see with issues such as increased resource guarding, inability to settle, skin issues and hyperactivity. This is often due to breeders accepting behavioural traits within dogs because they breed them for their colour and genes not for their temperament and health.
- The Bedlington Terrier x Whippet – because people tend to fall in love with their scrufty, tufty look which is very appealing to many. However, it is worth not losing sight of the fact that you are selecting a dog designed to chase (Whippet) and a dog designed to seek out and get hold of vermin (Bedlington Terrier). In other words, you're bringing home a dog that is designed to chase and kill small animals. Many owners, of course, will try to stop this behaviour because it isn't that desirable in the local park, but there is an argument that if a dog was created to do something, why would you take on a breed or crossbreed that you are going to spend all your time trying to change? If this behaviour would distress you, find a breed not created to chase, catch and kill, and you will be setting you and your puppy up for much more fun together.
- The Fox Red Labrador – being chosen more and more due to its colour rather than people understanding that the breed tends to be far better suited to working and being out in the field than just at home. Due

to their busy nature, they have a need to be out and about, wanting to be doing something. They are not a lazy Labrador that will sleep all day.

I could go on. I just wanted to flag some of the most common breeds and colours that I am seeing in my consultancy work and why selecting a dog on this basis isn't where we want to be. We need to take a much more in-depth approach to choosing the dog that joins us, as it makes the world of difference to the life we end up living with our dog.

Choosing the right breed is a combination of knowing what you, and anyone who lives with you, will be capable of in terms of exercise, time, attention, etc., and what the dog will need because of the nature of its breed. Both are equally important considerations, and I always advise clients to have thought carefully and done their research before making their decision about what breed or cross-breed of puppy to get.

Your puppy breed checklist

- What do I *want* to spend my time doing with the dog I live with? E.g. running every day, going to agility classes each weekend, playing in the garden with the kids, taking him to work or working from home while he snoozes in his basket, being able to do jobs with you while you potter around? We each have our own ideals, but being true to ourselves is key as well as asking each family member.

- What is the *least* amount of exercise I could do with the dog on a daily basis? Don't aim for your best options, as that isn't realistic, but aim for what is actually doable and probable every day of the week when you are working and have less time.
- What things do I really *love* about friends' and family's dogs that I know and have met? E.g. being cuddly, being able to pick them up on the bus, their desire to play.
- What things do I really *dislike* about family and friend's dogs that I know and have met? E.g. the barking at everything, the slobber, the inability to settle down.
- Does fur type impact your choice? E.g. how much they moult or the feel of the fur.
- What size dog would you like, while also remembering that size doesn't equal exercise needs? For example, a working-type Jack Russell will need more exercise than a Neapolitan Mastiff.
- How do you feel about barking? Some people love a dog who alert-barks, while others don't want a dog who barks at the door. It is worth considering this as barking can be such a big thing to try to solve or change when you could just choose a dog for whom this isn't their default behaviour, so you aren't fighting it.
- If you are looking at crossbreeds, do a really deep dive into the two breeds that are being crossed, as you don't know which bits you are going to get. The issues people are having with Cockapoos is the perfect example, as if you go and buy a working

Cocker Spaniel x Standard Poodle then this is going to be very, very different from a show-type Cocker crossed with a Toy Poodle.

The seven main breed groups

The best starting point when considering a particular puppy is to understand which of the main breed types that dog has been bred from. Dog breeding can be complicated, but there are seven primary breed groups that dogs are bred from, and having an understanding of what that dog was bred for and why will help you have an appreciation of what it might need from its owner. I don't necessarily agree with these groupings, but it is what the UK Kennel Club is based on. (I believe that the groupings need updating, with some dogs needing to move into other groups because their breed traits would be better suited, and this would then help owners make better decisions.)

Working Dogs

These tend to be dogs that were created and bred to a particular working job such as pulling a sled, defending land, police work and so on. These breeds are active and need to be kept busy. Examples of this kind of dog would be a Doberman, Great Dane and Boxer. You won't be able to stop them wanting to do their job, so you will need to figure out how you can channel this and how it will impact your life and home.

Gundog

These are dogs designed to work in the field and either hunt, point or retrieve. So they tend to be great at duration – they need a huge amount of walking, exercise and stimulation. They too need to have jobs factored into their daily life or else they will go self-employed. By self-employed, I mean that they will find their own ways of fulfilling their breed traits, e.g. going into the bushes, hunting, using their nose to follow scents you don't want them to, roaming far, as you aren't directing them. Examples of this kind of dog are the Working Cocker Spaniel, Labrador and Hungarian Vizsla.

Pastoral

Once again, we created this breed group to do one of three jobs – to herd, to move or to guard. These tend to be on farms with livestock, and they love being outside. They are hardy dogs who have had very specific traits bred into them, such as herding, so if they do not have an outlet for those traits it will be channelled into things you don't want, like herding and nipping at passing cars and children. Examples of this kind of dog are the Anatolian Shepherd, Border Collie and Welsh Corgi.

Terrier

A group often totally underestimated as many of this breed group can be small in size. However, terriers are mostly fearless, good at working alone, don't need direction and will just crack on and get the job done. So if you are looking for a dog who listens to your every word and wants your direction, the Terrier group isn't for you! Examples of this breed group would be the Patterdale Terrier and Jack Russell Terrier. Do bear in mind that the Staffordshire Bull Terrier is also in this group, which actually tends to have the exact opposite characteristics – they are heavily people dependent and actually want to be doing what you are doing!

Hound

The dogs in this breed group were made to use their nose or their eyes. These dogs are designed to explore, to be led by those senses, and that can often result in sprinting off, going underground and more. You won't be able to stop that breed requirement, so you will instead need to work with it. Examples of these breeds include Whippet, Dachshund, Greyhound and Beagle.

Utility

This grouping name is the least helpful in my opinion, as it includes dog breeds of all kinds designed to do a plethora of things, but each different! Examples of breeds in this category are the English Bulldog, the Boston Terrier and the Poodle. It makes zero sense to me!

Toy

Specifically bred for their size, ability to be handled, to be companions and to be with people. Once again, it doesn't make a lot of sense to me as a category, as there are breeds in here purely for their size, but their temperament and job mean they definitely aren't the most easy to handle or train. Take, for example, a Russian Toy Terrier, which is definitely a different kettle of fish from a Cavalier King Charles! Do not fall into the trap of believing that this category means any breed is suitable to be easy companion dogs, as they are not!

Rather than being swayed by an adorable photograph, or a puppy on your lap, ask yourself what was the dog *created* to do? Was it designed to be out all day in the field, to bark at rodents, to go down holes and catch vermin and kill them, to use their mouth and bite, to be on the go and work for long periods? This informs whether it matches your desires – if you dislike barking dogs, why would you choose a breed designed to be vocal?

You should also be checking if there are different *versions* of this breed – for example, a working type vs a show type. And if so, which might be best suited to what you want in life, e.g. a working Cocker Spaniel vs a show-type Cocker Spaniel are two very, very different breeds. Do watch out for breeders who say things like, 'A working type is well suited to family life', as that actually means a dog on a farm who is busy all day and comes in at night to be with the family. That is not the same as living in Manchester in an apartment with small kids and a dog that gets to go out on a couple of walks a day.

Ask yourself: can that breed live a healthy and happy life with me? And question *why* you think you could give a dog of a particular breed an excellent home. What will you be able to give that dog that will fulfil what it is bred to do? If you don't know that and can't answer it, you are going to struggle hugely.

I think it's useful to see some real-life examples of some of my clients, and how the breed they chose complemented the life of both the dog and the owner:

Penny the show x working Cocker Spaniel goes to work at their owner's warehouse in Sussex every day, where we incorporated scent work into their daily routine while on the premises. Penny lives in a city setting but goes to a countryside workplace every weekday, with access to acres of land for walks behind their warehouse.

Nottie the Hungarian Vizsla lives in east London right by the open marshlands, with access to water, forests and long grass for every single walk. Her owners moved home to get a larger garden for her to be able to sunbathe in and patrol for foxes.

Barry the Border Terrier loves to be out and about every day. He lives in a location where his owners can easily access huge parks while also being able to take him easily on the train to work with them in the office.

Dottie the Cavapoo was specifically chosen because she needed to be able to go to work with my client in her beauty business, and also to be able to collect the kids from school and go on runs three times a week around the Docklands area of London.

In order for every puppy, regardless of breed, to be happy you need to be able to supply:

- Daily exercise, excursions and outings that will suit your puppy's needs.

- Mental stimulation and training.
- Games and play.
- Interaction with you and your family.
- A feeling of safety and security.
- An environment where they will thrive and not just 'exist'.

Considering all of these factors when weighing up what you can offer as an owner, plus what your breed needs, is one of the single most important things you can do to set yourself up to succeed.

What each puppy needs from that list will differ to varying degrees. For example, a noise-sensitive Border Collie designed to herd all day long will hate busy roads and life in a city, and a working Cocker Spaniel that doesn't have access to stimulating environments to walk in will find life very hard.

Making these breed decisions is huge, and sometimes means admitting that the puppy you'd had your heart set on is not right for you at this moment in your life. But I swear that the effort and thought you put in now will pay dividends when you bring your puppy home and raise them to be the dog you want to share your life with.

A note on crossbreeds

We are now seeing many more crossbreeds that are being bred on purpose. Years ago, these would have been called mongrels, but now we are specifically breeding particular combinations and labelling them as the answer to people's allergy issues or moulting desires, but we do have to bear some things in mind. Such as:

- There is no such thing as a hypoallergenic dog. It doesn't exist. We may find certain pups in a litter may invoke less of a reaction, but that is dependent on the dog, and will vary within a litter. It certainly is not a 'trait' that we can rely on by simply getting a Cockapoo.
- Many crossbreeds display some of the worst behavioural issues I've encountered, and in my view this is largely due to their breeding. Cockapoos continue to be the main breed that I am contacted about, with reports of behavioural issues of fear, aggression, not having an 'off' switch and an inability to settle and relax – making some of them very hard to live with. All of this will come from the dogs they were bred from, how they were bred and what was used in order to get the curliest, cutest coat and colourways.
- If you are buying a crossbreed, you need to understand the breed traits of each breed that has been used to create the dog you are looking at. If, for example, you can't bear yappy dogs and you are looking at the Cavapoochon, then you really don't want to go for this combination!
- You will need to look at the differing health issues each breed can have and make sure you have done your due diligence in terms of health testing, scoring and outcomes, because many crossbreeds can dilute issues in some breeds but they can also cause other issues that you may not have thought about. For

example, if you were looking at a Cockapoo, we are already seeing that issues such as PRA (progressive retinal atrophy) that creates blindness comes from both parents. This can create more problems when we look at hip dysplasia, which is not controlled by a single gene but by many that work together to create the problem. Generally speaking, with a pedigree dog, in order to get Kennel Club approval prospective owners would expect to see evidence of health testing; whereas with crossbreeds, owners may not know they can ask for this, and not every breeder of crossbreeds will do these health tests as standard.

WHY THE PUPPY YOU CHOOSE IMPACTS YOUR LIFE

The reality is that the actual puppy you choose can make or break your future with that dog. So I want that decision to be one you make with confidence, feeling informed and prepared. And, ultimately, that it will ensure you will be happy together.

I always say to my clients, when selecting a puppy you have three things to remember:

- Choose the right breed for your lifestyle.
- Find the best breeder you can.
- Select the right puppy from that litter for you and your set-up.

And if you are looking at taking on a rescue puppy, then you still need to bear in mind that you need to:

- Understand where they have come from and the potential impact this may have.
- Examine breeds that may be within your dog and whether they feel right for you.
- Select the right puppy based on personality, temperaments and your experience of them.
- Find a rescue who is honest and provides proper assessments of the puppies they are rehoming.

With those three things sorted, you are already halfway towards having a happy relationship with your dog, for life!

When we are considering which puppy to choose there are some important further issues and common beliefs that you do need to bear in mind. They may not be deal-breakers for you, but it's crucial to understand what that choice may mean for you if you decide to ignore it.

If the mother rejected the litter

Maternal rejection will impact the dog your puppy grows into. They will have spent their first weeks of life without their mum's crucial input in their primary socialisation period. Do look at who raised the litter. For instance, did a relative of the mother step in (e.g. a grandmother) or were they raised by the breeder on the bottle? A lack of maternal input cannot be ignored. Without a mother to teach them about boundaries, like stopping them when they are biting her, this can and will impact their abilities to interact with other dogs. They will not have learned this while in their imprinting stage, so we may see more likelihood of reactivity towards other dogs; an inability to understand boundaries or being told not to do something as there was no mother to show them; or a lack of confidence around dogs. These aren't issues to underestimate and brush over. On the flipside, this might not be an issue for you if you live in a remote place and there are no visiting dogs, so a people focus is more than fine for your life. It may also not be so much of an issue if they were taken in or raised by another kind adult bitch who showed them the way and they had other adult dogs in the home to learn from that were great examples.

If there is only one puppy born/surviving

Having been an only pup doesn't need to be a problem, but it will depend on the breeder and how the puppy was raised. The puppy won't have had its littermates to learn from, which can be problematic if it isn't living with other dogs. If, however, the puppy is raised within a home where there are other supportive, kind, considerate dogs and they get involved in teaching and raising the puppy, then it can lead to a puppy being very well rounded as it gets so much of the mother's input from them. Plus, the elder dogs who it will learn to play with will lead to your puppy learning to adapt its style of interaction depending on who it is playing with. You sometimes find that these dogs mature more quickly because the way they were raised was almost fast tracked.

Believing that all puppies in the litter are the same

Even if a breeder tells you that they are pretty similar, there will still be differences between each puppy in the litter. Each pup has their own way of doing things, and figuring out the one that will suit you best is of the utmost importance. For example, there may be one that just sits and observes and likes to wander off and do things alone, and there may be one that likes to bother the others in the litter. Choosing the one you feel fits your life is going to be important: the observer could be great for a home that already has an older dog in it, whereas the one who bothers all the puppies will be your older dog's worst nightmare, and that would not be fair.

Thinking that a puppy 'chose you'

I'm afraid I tend to disagree when people tell me this happened. In the majority of cases, it simply will have been the pushiest puppy which got past the littermates and onto your lap. And a pushy puppy can work for some people but, for many, it isn't the puppy they should be choosing. Pushy doesn't mean best suited, so really think about what kind of personality you want from your puppy that will turn into an adult dog, especially if you already have another dog in the home.

Choosing the nervous one because it looks sad

In a well-bred litter, there shouldn't be a puppy exhibiting anxious or nervous behaviour, as they should have been bred from a confident and happy mother and raised in a kind and caring setting. Taking on the most nervous, scared dog is definitely not a wise choice for the vast majority of people unless you want to actively spend a huge amount of time figuring out how to build confidence and raise a dog that doesn't live its life in fear. A client bought a puppy who was petrified, shaking, wouldn't make eye contact, was hiding and desperately trying to not be seen and touched – and the 'breeder' convinced her it was all fine. This puppy went on to be put to sleep before it was two years old due to severe behavioural and medical complications that meant this dog could not integrate into a human world and actually became a danger to society.

Making a decision based on sex, colour or pattern of fur

Please, just don't do this. If any breeder asks you to choose from the litter over the phone based on a colour and sex, hang up. Any breeder who will allow you to make a decision on superficial grounds, rather than selecting the most suitable puppy for your circumstances, is one who should be avoided. This also applies to adverts: if the breeder is charging more for a certain colour, that is not a breeder you want to be involved with.

Is the mother a dog you'd want to take home?

Lastly, the mother (the bitch) you see in with the litter should be a dog that you would gladly take home. Is she friendly? Anxious? Engaged with humans? Her behaviour should be indicative of a dog you would like to share your life with, and if it isn't, then that breeder and that litter is not the right one for you and the search continues. What happens when those puppies are *in utero*, first born and being raised by the mother is so deeply ingrained – and part of their genetics and imprinting – that we as humans simply cannot undo it.

CHOOSE YOUR BREEDER CAREFULLY

If you feel you have chosen your breed or crossbreed and you feel thoroughly comfortable and prepared, then finding a breeder is the next step. And this is where you can start to feel disillusioned. The breeding of dogs has exploded into a gigantic money-making business for many, many people and that makes it much harder to weed out the great breeders breeding great dogs from puppy farmers, puppy dealers, backyard breeders and scammers.

So many well-intentioned dog owners end up unwittingly buying a dog from a puppy farm, or a dubious seller of some kind. I'm going to give you a thorough checklist to ensure that you don't go through the heartbreaking experience of bringing home a puppy with severe health or behavioural issues. I know it's hard to walk away from a puppy you've fallen in love with, but buying from unscrupulous breeders only encourages them to breed more puppies in dire conditions.

To be a breeder within the UK you can be anyone – and I do mean anyone – so always have that at the forefront of your mind. You could be buying a living baby animal from someone who has no interest in, no education in and no knowledge of how to breed or raise a puppy. You could be buying and taking that dog into your home and expecting it to just turn out OK. You can start to see how things go so terribly wrong.

It's OK, this breeder is licensed

Within the UK, a licensed breeder is not a guarantee of best practice. It simply means that the person has a licence to breed three or more litters of puppies in any twelve-month period, and sell any of them on – it could license them for eighty breeding dogs, or one. You can look up their license number via their local council to see how many dogs they are licensed to breed from, however, they may be breeding from multiple dogs but say they are only breeding from a few; it's worth a look anyway. Applicants for licences must satisfy certain conditions regarding their premises and conduct, and any licence granted is subject to renewal. Only those with animal welfare convictions are ineligible for a licence, and there are fines in place for those who breach licence terms.

There is no affix, accreditation or scheme that you can trust implicitly as a symbol that your dog is being bred in a decent, ethical and kind manner. Many of these licensing or accreditation schemes will carry out visits but breeders are sometimes warned when a visit is happening and, in my view, the checks are not conducted frequently enough, often only happening every few years.

This breeder is part of the breed council, so they're legit

By all means research the breed council for your chosen breed and talk to the secretary and the person responsible for ensuring the health of puppies bred as this breed, but be aware: these are not always independent voices.

It looks good on the internet!

Third-party sales sites are exactly that: a site that allows anyone to upload and advertise their litter for a fee. There are terms and conditions for placing ads on these sites, but users are neither vetted nor checked. Anyone can upload images, videos and write anything that they like about themselves, their breeding and their set-up. You should be aware of the possibility that some sellers might lie about health checks, assessments and temperaments of the dogs they bred from – so it will be down to you to weed these people out. That can take a huge amount of time, brain power and heartache.

But I follow them online, and they seem great!

You can now use social-media sites like TikTok and Instagram to search for dogs and puppies, even though the sale of live animals is not permitted on these sites. Celebs and influencers will also tag kennels and breeders that they used. Don't forget, they can be gifted a free puppy to get them to do this. Which is extremely worrying in itself. And with many of these known names having zero knowledge about puppies and dogs, their influence should not be something that sways you.

It's OK, this puppy is from a friend of a friend

It used to be the case that someone knew someone whose dog had had puppies, and off you went to see the litter. It can be a nice way to find a breeder, but you still need to vet them in the same way you would if you were cold-calling a breeder you found online. It's a bit like when a friend has recommended a restaurant or hotel and you get there and wonder what on earth they were on about. The same is true of people recommending a breeder. Just because it worked for them doesn't mean it will for you.

The good breeder checklist

First things first, you need to be identifying breeders who are creating the kind of puppy you are looking for. This sounds obvious, but you would be shocked at how many people fall at his hurdle. If you would like a dog to be a part of your family, it should be raised like that by the breeder, in a family environment with children around. If you are looking to get a working-line Labrador, then you would be looking for a breeder who works her Labs and is specifically breeding for working excellence and personality. These things matter: you can't get a dog bred for farm work and expect it to be happy in a city.

Let's assume that you have identified a couple of breeders that you like the look of. Your next step is to have a conversation with them. It can feel overwhelming figuring out where to start, what to ask and to know what to look for. With that in mind, I've made you some prompts and scripts to help you out. Of course, you don't have to follow these to the letter, but I'm using these to show how I might start, and then the kinds of questions you want to be asking.

For the purpose of this exercise, let us pretend that I am looking to add a calm, biddable Labrador to my family. In this scenario, I have two children, aged ten and twelve, and, while I have a decent garden, we live in a market town but have access to the nearby countryside.

> Hi there, I'm looking to speak to Julie as I understand she breeds Labradors . . .

> Oh, hi, Julie, I found your details on XXX and would love to find out a bit more. I'm in no rush but am searching to find a brilliant Labrador puppy to join our family.

> We have two kids who are aged ten and twelve, but the most important thing is trying to find a puppy from a calm and happy mother. Would it be OK to find out more about your litter and your situation, please?

Let them fill you in, then ask your follow-up questions below. Try to work these into the chat rather than firing questions one after the other, as that won't build a relationship! You are looking to be interested in the breeder's answers and allow them to question you. (It is a red flag if they don't, as they should be invested in finding the best possible homes for their puppies.) The aim of this call is to decide whether they are worth further communication and a visit.

QUESTIONS ABOUT THE BREEDER:

- **How long have you been breeding for?**
  Then google to see if what they say is true.
- **Do you breed any other breeds? If so, what? Are they breeds that are compatible personality-wise with the type of dog you are wanting to get?**
  Dogs are social learners and will learn from the other dogs around them, which is why this is important.
- **Where are you based?**
  Get a rough location, e.g. village name, and you can then google to see if their name comes up in any local press to see if it's true.
- **Are you a professional breeder or is this a family pet?**
  Try to dig deeper to see if breeding is their main income, or if they have another job and do this on the side. Is it their first litter? If they have another job, try to get an idea what it is, as all of this is useful for follow-up Google searches to see if what they are telling you marries up with what you can find online.

ABOUT THE MOTHER:

- **What is her personality like?**
  Listen out for descriptions that could indicate any tricky traits, e.g. she follows me everywhere, doesn't like to be left, barks at strangers, doesn't like new people, doesn't go out much, puts all the other dogs in their place. These are little phrases indicating there is underlying anxiety, stress, worry and fear.

- **What kind of exercise does she get each day?**
  For example, two hours a day on the beach plus going to the stables, or not long walks but they live on a twenty-acre farm so they are out and about heaps. Can you provide a puppy with a similar level of activity? Always clarify the details as one person's version of normal is not someone else's.
- **Has she had a litter before?**
  If so, ask for information on the previous litter, so you can see how they have turned out and the kinds of homes they are in. For example, if you search for them on Instagram and find all the puppies are in agility homes or working field trials, you will be able to see that they aren't the chilled-out family pet you are searching for. You can even ask if they have a Facebook group for previous litters that you can look at or engage with.
- **Does the mother have any allergies? If so, to what?**
  You may need to dig deeper and ask more in person, regarding things like: recurring ear infections, dusty fur, constantly itching, weeping eyes, chewing at paws. If a dog with allergies has been bred from, you need to consider the possibility of vulnerabilities being passed on to your puppy, as well as what medication they are on and the impact *in utero*.
- **Could you send me some videos and pictures of the mother in everyday life?**

ABOUT THE FATHER:

- Ask similar questions as above but about why they decided to use him as a stud.

- If they own him, then you should be able to meet him and apply the same criteria and questions as you did to the mother.

ABOUT THE LITTER:

- **How many are there and did any die?**
- **How would the breeder describe the litter and the individual puppies – are they able to describe their differences and nuances?**
  A decent breeder should be in with those puppies every day, and they should be able to give you infinite details about each puppy. If they can't or won't, there is an issue.
- **How are the puppies being raised and who is in the house with them?**
  This is to check that they are in the home and not in a shed or outbuilding. If you're buying a farm dog that will live in heated kennels, then an outbuilding is fine, but if you want a dog that is comfortable with living in a family home, it should have spent its first weeks in a family home. Remember a breeder can 'tell' you anything, but it's up to you to find out if it's true.
- **Do the puppies live with any other dogs?**
  If so, what and find out about them and their personalities.
- **Do the puppies live with any other pets like a cat/ horses/on a farm, and what exposure have the puppies had with them?**
- **What are they being fed? And how are they fed?**
  Ask if the breeder uses a bowl for each puppy or if

they are fed out of one bowl. The latter can increase the likelihood of resource-guarding issues later on. You can also look out for this on photos of the puppies and how they are being fed. Ask for images and videos so you can see the set-up of where the puppies spend most of their time.

- **Do the puppies have access to different surfaces? (Important for toilet training.)**
- **Do they have lots of toys and things to mouth on? (Important for building resilience and interest.)**
- **Do they have access to different rooms in the house or the garden? (Great for creating curious puppies.)**

ABOUT HEALTH CHECKS CARRIED OUT BEFORE BREEDING:

- **Which health checks were done before breeding? E.g. hips/elbows/PRA (progressive retinol atrophy) for eyes which can result in blindness.**
  If you are unsure, go to the breed-council website and look at what health certificates and checks should have been done. (You can google 'German Shorthaired Pointer Breed Council' and the country you live in, and write down a list of ranges of scores or ideal answers so that you can gauge the risk factors from what they are saying. Remember, anyone can say anything over the phone!
- **Can you provide me with real and original paperwork if I visit?**
  Ask if they can show you and allow you to check its authenticity, as paperwork is pretty easy to falsify.

Don't just take their word for it, make a note of the names on it and then google or talk to the testing centre to make sure they all marry up. You would be amazed at how easy it is to buy false paperwork online.

The puppy culture method

In my opinion, some of the best breeders are using the Puppy Culture method to raise their litter. This is an American standard that is based on raising happy, calm, resilient, curious puppies who can slot into family life very easily. It is an incredible system that walks breeders through every step from birth until the day the puppies leave.

If you would like to understand more to feel better equipped about what you are looking for in a breeder, you can purchase the Puppy Culture breeder folder online. This folder will give you a huge insight into the work the breeder should and could be doing in order to create excellent dogs to be a part of society. You will also really see and notice the difference between those who are using it and those who aren't. And the reason is because this folder of work has been designed to provide breeders with tasks, ways of raising the puppies, socialisation schedules, resilience training and much more. So any breeder using this method should go to the top of your list, and you should really be able to see the evidence of the method in real life by the conversations you are having with them, the images you receive, the videos you see and feedback on the puppies in the litter you are enquiring about.

How to spot a puppy farm/puppy mill

I wrote about this in great detail in my first book, and I flag it often via social media. Many people are surprised to learn that puppy farms exist within the UK. As a country, we are utterly failing dogs by allowing these types of establishments to continue. More than that, we are actively creating a problem for every person and family who lives with one of these dogs, and the impact on society is an even bigger issue: just look at rehoming centre numbers, dog bites, dog attacks and allergy issues for dogs.

In case you aren't sure what makes a breeder a puppy farm/mill, let me give you a bit more detail on what these two things are before we look at how they are conning you.

A puppy farm or puppy mill is an establishment that breeds puppies, and lots of them, of varying breeds and keeps them in poor conditions. They often hide behind social-media profiles that look professional, but essentially they are created by money-grabbing owners who raise dogs in dire conditions and sell them on at a large profit. These puppies are simply a commodity – their health, welfare, condition, mental health, and suitability for your family are not the reasons for breeding: money is. These breeders are making a lot of money each year from breeding bitches who are kept in terrible conditions. Raising the puppies in appalling conditions is the constant cycle of their business.

The puppy farms find their customers in several ways:

- They advertise via a third-party website, and they go between them all. Some even have their own websites too.

- They will run the farms from varying locations, some small and some large. If they sell puppies from their premises, they will bring the dogs up to the front garden or the kitchen to show them to you when they visit, with the actual breeding areas hidden out of sight. But you may hear other dogs or, if you look on Google Maps, you may see that the address has lots of outbuildings, and this is a red flag. There is one puppy farm I know that allows you into the actual breeding pens, so they are not even attempting to hide it. They are concrete cells with sawdust.
- They will rent puppies out to yoga classes using them for puppy yoga for a profit. Please avoid this practice, which is not created with the puppy's welfare in mind.
- They will pass them to a puppy dealer who will show them to prospective buyers in their home or a house they have rented for a few days. Once they have been seen and deposits have been put down, the puppies will be returned to the breeding kennels or farm to live back in squalor, where they barely see the light of day until the day you pick them up.
- They will pass the ones that don't sell, who are perhaps too ill or they bred too many of, to rescue centres who will then sell them on as a rescue from a breeder, or they may even simply kill them. I did some work for a TV show which went undercover and was shown puppy-farm facilities, including puppies who had been killed and simply piled into black bin bags. It is hard to read but important you understand the types of people we are talking about.

- Some farms or mills will have breeding bitches in neater conditions, like a huge row of kennels, rather like the battery farming of chickens. It is still the same issue, though – dogs that are not socialised, well-adjusted or used to being a part of everyday family life, and this has huge repercussions for the puppies they are birthing.

Aside from the welfare of the dogs and puppies, there are a few other things to bear in mind about puppy farms.

- These establishments often have criminal backgrounds and can be involved in crime in some other ways.
- These dogs are not 'bred well', as in they are not bred for temperament, nature and personality, so this can cause huge issues behaviourally when they land in people's homes.
- The puppies and their mothers have zero socialisation, human contact and links to the human world. That will have a gigantic impact on the dog you bring home and its lack of ability to integrate, enjoy and thrive in the world we want them to live in.
- The puppies are often bred so badly that they will have either medical issues for life, e.g. gastro problems, allergies, ear infections. Or, in the most extreme cases, they will have to be put to sleep due to their medical, behavioural or neurological issues.
- These puppy-mill owners are creating a business based on pain, deprivation and maximising income. None of these are the foundations you want when buying a dog.

Many of my clients have felt sorry for a puppy when visiting. They didn't feel like they could leave that dog behind, so they brought it home to save it. By doing this, in honesty, you are paving the way for the next horrifically bred puppy to go into the system. If we stop the demand, we stop the breeding. When you think about it, there is actually a very easy way to get rid of these awful people and that is to stop buying from them. But in order to do that, together we need to educate the world on how to spot these unscrupulous dealers and not go through with buying these dogs, however much we would like to save them. Spread the word, and ensure that you, and those you love, understand how to avoid farmed puppies.

Reporting a puppy farm

If you do visit a 'breeder' or dealer and you feel it is a puppy farm, then you should report them to the council they are licensed under, to the RSPCA and potentially even to HMRC if you have concerns over how they are asking for payment. In addition, you can report the premises to the police if you feel there are criminal activities going on. A client of mine turned up to a home to view a litter of puppies and there were bodyguards there. That isn't normal!

Do bear in mind that many dealers and farmers thrive by making things look 'normal' and boring. Perhaps in a house that could be anyone's, on a cul de sac that could be a family home, on a farm where they tell you the barking you hear is the neighbour's dogs. They will tell you the mum of the litter is out for a walk hence why you can't see her. Or that the daughter is showing you the litter as her mum has had to go into hospital so couldn't be around to meet you despite you chatting to her on the phone and WhatsApp. In 90 per cent of my clients' cases with puppy-farm dogs, those kinds of excuses have always been used to hide the truth.

Show breeders can run puppy farms

There are some show breeders who will keep their breeding bitches crated, focusing on colour and look above all else, breeding too many of them, accepting personality traits that should not be bred from in order to get the best colour or conformation according to the standards that the Kennel Club lay out for showing. I'll never forget visiting a litter of red Poodle puppies and finding out the mother had been bred from despite her being aggressive and difficult towards people – the breeder wanted her colour and conformation over everything else. Kennel Club-assured breeders can only breed from dogs which have been appropriately health screened, but their breed standards are there for the look, the conformation, the structure, the fur and the posture of the dog. This can result in some breeders focusing on the look of the dog, instead of their temperament. Can you imagine if, instead of the look of the dog, we had standards that had very clear temperament and personality requirements, to ensure our breeders were forced to breed brilliant, well-rounded, happy puppies and dogs – or else they would lose out and be penalised? It would transform dog breeding for ever.

When you are doing your due diligence on your breeder, there is never a way of knowing 100 per cent if they are breeding dogs with the best intentions. It just isn't possible. But doing that due diligence with the information above may help you weed out the breeders who are acting in bad faith.

I advise my clients, as I advise you, that as someone looking to buy a puppy you should work on the assumption that there will be an issue with a breeder and try to prove to yourself that there isn't. This feels negative, but it is the best way to ensure you bring home a puppy that will easily settle into your home as a much-loved family pet.

CONSIDERATIONS FOR TAKING ON A RESCUE PUPPY

Due to the ways that we are breeding and choosing dogs, rescue centres are overrun with brilliant dogs needing brilliant homes. The perception that every dog in rescue has an issue is ill founded. We see puppies and dogs that are in there due to no fault of their own, because owners did none of the things I've listed above and so chose the wrong puppy, or the wrong breed, and ended up having to get rid of it because they realised they had made a huge mistake. There are also many puppies in rescue that are either being brought across from other countries or that have been born in rehoming centres due to a mother that was pregnant being abandoned.

I would strongly urge you to investigate the world of rescue, there are brilliant people and rescues doing wonderful things. And then there are some that are not doing quite so well – so just as you would when looking for a breeder, you do need to be looking at rescues in the same light. You need to be finding ones that will vet you, allocate dogs to the right homes and avoid the ones that will just ship a dog over from a foreign country because you paid a deposit online or because you said you wanted that puppy on their website. The same thing applies – in order for you to have a happy life with a rescue puppy, you need to have chosen well, done your research, thought about every prospective issue and considered breed, trauma, experience and age of the puppy. So with that in mind, while this list cannot be exhaustive (that could be a book on its own), here are some topline areas to think about, ask about and consider . . .

Why is the puppy you are looking at in rescue?

Much like looking at a mother when you visit a breeder, understanding how a puppy was raised is still important information for you to get hold of and understand. It will impact your puppy and the life you have together. With rescues, it may be that the puppy was taken on by a family who adored and doted on it, but soon realised that they did not have the time that the Springer Spaniel puppy needed. You may be able to find out how long the puppy was in the original family, roughly where they lived (town vs rural) and what kind of household it went into. You may be able to figure out its confidence and personality rather like you do when visiting a litter. This would be very different from a puppy that comes from a street-dog mother who has always lived on the street and is fearful of people and therefore reactive to them. That dog may have had their litter in a rehoming centre where the puppies are not socialised, exposed or given more than the food and water needed to survive. I cannot lie and pretend that these things don't matter. They do. The trauma the mother goes through impacts our puppies *in utero*, as does the cortisol (the stress hormone) they repeatedly receive because of the stress of situations. It impacts the way those puppies come into the world. And the way that those puppies view the world. So of course we want to help those dogs and those puppies, but you also have to be certain that the puppy you are taking on is one that you truly feel equipped to bring up. Just in the same way as I stated earlier about finding the right breed and personality when you are looking at a breeder, these key things are critical and we cannot and should not just gloss over them when considering a rescue puppy. For me, the more prepped, the more informed and the more ready you are, the better your journey with your puppy will be!

Think about the age and stage of the puppy you are looking at

We often think that the age of the puppy we are considering in rescue is irrelevant, but it isn't. This is rather like when a client contacts me to tell me that they are getting a puppy from a breeder at four months old. 'Why?' I always ask. The reason I do so is because you need to understand that you, as the owner, will have missed out on the secondary socialisation period – the critical period where we introduce our puppy to the life they are going to live with us, where we provide exploration, association and input that is going to shape our lives together. If someone else has been in control of that period, you need to know what that has involved or else you may encounter issues later on due to what they experienced. More on ages and stages later.

What kind of care has the puppy been receiving?

Think about whether the puppy has been in foster care with some amazing role-model dogs, or if it has it been sat alone in a rescue centre with very few resources. Each rescue centre differs, so understanding what the puppy has had access to is critical. Has it been in a rehoming centre filled with barking, stressed-out dogs for the whole of its life up until you see it? Whatever experience it has had is important to factor in and think about, as it will impact the puppy during its imprinting stage. (More on this on page 27, where I also discuss single puppies.) We will never truly know what has the greater impact – nature vs nurture – but what we do know is that both matter. So considering what they have or have not had and where they are at now is important. I want you and your puppy to have a great life together, so considering all of this is critical. Let me give you a couple of examples.

I fostered a tiny abandoned Staffy-type puppy who was dumped at a police station in north London. We named him Teddy. At the time, I had a deaf English Bulldog called Cookie and he looked to her as his role model: he copied her when out, he watched her every move (she was the kindest dog ever). The puppy came out with me on training walks and I carried him everywhere as a baby! He met my client's dogs that were suitable for him to learn from, and he was in our home – we cooked for him, played with him, gave him brilliant experiences and eventually found him a loving home with a couple. But he ended up having to go and live with the owner's parents in the remote countryside, as he was so reactive to dogs and people that he had to be muzzled every time he went out of the house. He had to have a pen built within their kitchen where he could be kept if workmen came over or if there were visitors. With his inner circle he was a totally different dog. He is an old man now and happily living out his retirement because his owner's parents are incredibly understanding, and also have a big countryside property where he can be kept safely away from people. They have a pool where he can swim and land that he can roam, knowing he will not encounter strangers or unknown dogs. I tell this tale because I don't know what happened to him before I fostered him – I don't know who his parents were, who his breeder was, who he was raised by initially and what experiences he had, what he saw or felt – but we can see it all subsequently had a gigantic effect on him. We have to keep an open mind to understand the complexity of our dogs when it comes to breeding and nurturing, not just believe that loving a dog can cure all. We have to be open, honest and realistic in choosing the right puppy to join us.

On the flipside to this, I once had a client with a bull breed who she found tied up to a bench in the snow. She took him home and contacted me and I advised her from day dot what to do and where to do things, as he was about six weeks old at the time. We don't know his background, what happened to him or what he was bred from, but I do know that he turned out to be an utter legend of a dog. He could have been a pets-as-therapy dog if his owners had wanted him to be. Once again, I'll never know what played the biggest role – nature or nurture – but we do have to have one eye on all these things so that we can try to make the best decisions and choices to set up our dogs to succeed to the best of our abilities. That is all that we can do.

Is the breed or breed combo the right one for you?

If you have gone via a breed-specific rescue, you will be pretty sure what the breed is, but if you have found a dog where you don't have access to that information, you need to think about a few things. If you don't know what the breed or breed combo is, then you need to look at the way the dog does things: how they play, what they are interested in, what they want to spend their time doing. These things will be what helps you ascertain whether these are attributes you like and want in a dog or not. You don't want to take on a Malinois cross that enjoys jumping fences, can clear river banks and wants to be doing heel training a few hours a day, when all you were looking for was a hang-out companion that could come to work with you, play in the house and do two shorter walks a day!

I took on a foster dog called Mr Happy Henry. We fostered him for six months and he was incredible. I made a guess at what he was breed-wise after those months of living with him, playing with him and training him, because you couldn't tell from his looks. He ran and played like a Boxer (he had so much energy, loved to leap, to bound, to learn, had an incredible nose and could box like a Boxer), he had the lovability, stature and short attention span of a Great Dane, and the docile parts of a Mastiff when at home after having been walked. I never did a test on him but instead I looked at what and how he did things to ascertain breed traits to help me find the right home for him.

Ask tons of questions about what the rescue puppy likes to do, how they do it, and if they have videos, so that you can start to make some decisions for yourself. Bear in mind, many rescue centres can't give you reliable info on things like how much exercise and stimulation the dog might need, as they themselves cannot provide it – as they are a rescue, trying to keep a lot of dogs alive, safe and looked after is their most important day-to-day task. The dog may be getting only an hour in a paddock a day and surviving on that, because that is the only option in their situation. It doesn't mean when it lands with you that will be enough.

Decent assessments are key

The last thing to say on rescues is that if you are considering going down the rescue route, you need to believe that the assessments the rescue is doing on the puppies are decent. That can feel like a big ask, so here is what I mean: when you read their blurb and look at how they are describing the dog you are looking at, it should be well

EVERYTHING YOUR PUPPY WANTS YOU TO KNOW

thought out, helpful information. It should mention what they know about the puppy, what kind of home they feel it is best suited to and why. All dogs should have been assessed and you are within your rights to ask who assessed the dog and when. Some rescues use volunteers to 'assess' dogs with no behavioural experience whatsoever, and this really is downright dangerous. The same is true when you look at dogs on third-party websites – anyone can say anything. You need to do as much of a deep dive as you do with breeders when it comes to rescues, which pop up all the time on social media and online market places.

Always find out more, ask and ask again – and take your time. This puppy needs to be the right fit for you and you need to be prepped on what the potential challenges are going to be, like with any puppy you take on.

CHAPTER TWO

Preparing to Bring Your Puppy Home

SHOPPING FOR YOUR PUPPY

You've chosen your puppy, and now you're ready to bring it home. It is tempting, if you have the budget, to go out and buy all the fancy beds, collars, toys and training games. If you don't have the budget, you might worry that you're unable to afford something essential. There is a whole industry built around telling you that your puppy absolutely needs a 'calming' bed despite it being no different from many other beds! You probably already know by now what I'm going to tell you: your puppy is an individual! It will have its own particular needs and preferences when it comes to how it sleeps and plays. However, there are a few things that will make a puppy's arrival in your home smoother, and some things you definitely don't need to spend money on!

On the following pages is my list of what you will need and should purchase, borrow or buy second hand, as well as my list of things you can save your money on. If you buy anything second hand or borrow it from another owner, just make sure you have washed and aired it sufficiently so that it doesn't smell of the other dog; have it in your home a few weeks before bringing the puppy home, so it settles and absorbs your home's scent.

What you actually need to buy for your puppy's arrival

Feeding

A bowl to eat out of that can be easily washed daily: Bear in mind that many dogs and puppies can be fearful of reflections in metal bowls, and that plastic bowls are often very light and move around a lot, so puppies may pick them up and chew or knock them over. For my own dogs, I prefer ceramic bowls. I've found you can pick up amazing vintage bowls in charity and thrift stores that are ideal and easy to pop in the dishwasher. They aren't 'dog bowls' but will serve just as well. Or you can buy specific brands like Mason & Cash that have stood the test of time, are heavy in weight, deep and can't be picked up by a curious puppy. I also have enamel bowls that my dog loves eating out of.

Two water bowls: One for outside in the garden and one for inside the house. I tend to avoid using plastic as I don't think it's a good thing for all of us, including our dogs. If you have more than one dog, then I always have more than one bowl of water e.g. two in the house and two in the garden so there never needs to be competition.

A rubber kids' placemat: Perfect for using on the floor to give your puppy different food outside of its bowl, such as trying out things like berries, peas, or a piece of spaghetti. Plus, some pups love eating from a flat surface so this works well if they're not used to a bowl yet, and you can just wipe it down afterwards. Make sure it has a lip at the edges so food can't roll off it. Or, if your dog prefers eating off the mat in general, you can feed him all his meals on it and then just wash it down or put it in the dishwasher.

A textured rubber mat and/or bowl: These tend to have patterns on which you spread peanut butter or other similarly spreadable food (even dog food). It takes some concentration and effort for your pup to access the food from the textured mat, and is great for tiring them out.

Sleeping

I recommend at least two dog beds – more if you have a house with lots of rooms that your dog will move between! Avoid cushion beds or the cheap nylon fabric ones sold on some social media sites. Choose beds that are supportive, comfortable, have washable elements and cater for many different sleeping styles.

Over the years I've found that there are some styles of sleeping that give us some interesting information on how your dog is feeling, and here are just a few examples, using my own terminology:

- The bagel: This is when your dog is curled up and looks like a bagel! This position is mostly showing us that your puppy is cold, doesn't feel secure or is wary around their surroundings, so can't fully relax.
- The pancake: When your dog lays flat on their side and goes into a deep sleep (showing that they feel relaxed and fulfilled enough to sleep).
- The bored sleep: Where they lay on their tummy snoozing but are ready to get up and go at a moment's notice. This isn't a deep sleep position but one where they are waiting. You often see dogs doing this next to desks, when they are waiting patiently for their owner to finish something and then take them out.

You will find that different breeds can also have different ways of resting and sleeping. For example, a Whippet tends to want to be very warm and wrapped up, a Greyhound loves to stretch and lay on their back with their legs akimbo, and a Dachshund will often start out curled up due to their long body but will unfurl quite quickly when they are comfortable.

So, when we look at beds you do need to be thinking about how your dog likes to sleep. If you are buying a circle-shaped bed and your dog wants to stretch out fully, then they either won't use the bed you buy or they will constantly be trying to get onto the sofa to stretch out!

As well as the bed itself, consider:

Other soft areas: A folded duvet, padded bath mat or blanket can be put on the floor when you identify somewhere your pup likes to flop down, but where you don't want to place an actual bed.

Bed padding: Soft toys or a baby duvet with a washable cover to pad their bed out, so that they feel cosy and like they are touching something and leaning on something to fall asleep with. It helps to remember that your puppy will have come from a litter where the puppies will have slept leaning on each other, so make sure you have options for your puppy to recreate that feeling. You can even roll up big towels and use those for your puppy to lean against or to help fill up their sleeping space. You can buy toys that can be heated, specifically designed to go in beds with puppies. However, be careful about using hot water bottles as these can be punctured by teeth and claws, and the same is true of wheat bags that you heat in microwaves.

Travelling in the car

When you are travelling with your dog in the car, they must be restricted so that they cannot cause harm, injure themselves or distract the driver. You have a few options for doing this.

Crate: If your dog is OK in a crate, then you can use one in the boot or on the back seat, strapped in.

Dog guard: These go behind the back seats so that your dog can have the freedom of the boot but not get into the back seats.

Harness attachment: These often come with a box for your puppy to sit in while safely anchored by the seat-belt attachment. This is great for puppies who want to sit up front with you.

Pet carrier: These can be used, but not one where their head can stick out the front so everyone can touch and fiddle with them. This is intrusive and annoying for the puppy and can cause behavioural issues later on.

Mat: For when you get to your destination, a padded memory-foam bathmat is useful, as it can be rolled up and washed easily, plus is suitable to be used in a cafe, pub or someone's house to help them settle down comfortably. It is worth bearing in mind that some small dogs, and ones with very thin fur, will find it difficult to settle on a hard floor, particularly if it is cold. Be prepared and you will save ages trying to settle the puppy when you're out.

At home

Baby gates: These are a must. If your breed will be tall, purchase the extra-tall ones. Very small puppies can easily squeeze through the bars of some stair gates, so you may need to reinforce this with mesh or wire until they get bigger. Make sure there are no spiky edges that your puppy can hurt or cut themselves on. They do need to be able to see through, so don't use things like cardboard.

A pen: If you would like to section off an area or have a spot to put your puppy while it has a chew or a raw bone, or if there are kids running around. If your puppy is very small, you can even use a cardboard box lined with a blanket. You will still need to make sure that people aren't going in, grabbing and pulling the puppy out of the box, as we are looking to create a safe, happy space.

Rugs: It may seem cute or funny, but your puppy slipping and sliding on slippery floors is to be avoided! The little slips – with back legs splayed, running and slipping – are actions that can end up damaging your puppy's development and condition in the long term. Buy rugs that line the hallway, place them in areas your puppy will be, and ensure they're situated near sofas and beds so that if the puppy tries to jump up they have grip. There are loads of companies that now sell washable rugs and these are great, as they are designed to go in the washing machine, which is ideal for puppyhood.

Steps: To put by the sofa or bed if you have high furniture, as we do not want puppies jumping up onto and off things constantly. This can damage their growing bones and cause long-term issues. Or you can make steps out of books!

A decent spray cleaner: To clean areas that have been toileted on, to make sure the scent is totally removed and avoid repeat marking. Do bear in mind that surfaces heavily impact where dogs choose to toilet (more on that in my previous book). Avoid highly perfumed and chemical versions as it just isn't great for anyone to ingest. I tend to just use an environmentally friendly bio laundry detergent that is safe for children and pets. Mix it up with water and have it in a spray bottle to use and mop with.

For walking

A puppy collar: It should be soft, lightweight and with a small tag on it with your details on. I tend to recommend that you don't put their name on the tag, so that others don't know the dog's name. Instead, put on as many phone numbers as you can fit, your house number and postcode/zip code, so that your dog can be returned if found and you and your partner or family are contactable. There have been situations where dogs have been lost when an owner is away, so do make sure that if your dog is staying with someone else, e.g. your parents or a dog minder, that while they are there you add a tag with their information on.

A 2m lead: I advise not getting a lead any shorter than that and don't use the flexi leads if you can avoid it (see page 67 for why I don't recommend them). This is the lead you will use most on the street or in busy environments, where you need to keep your dog close.

A 5m long line: This should be made from soft fabric that won't rip your hands to shreds when your puppy bolts! You can buy Biothane ones now that are waterproof, easy to wipe down and nice to hold. This is a lead you will use on walks every single day, from tiny puppyhood into teenagehood (when your puppy is ignoring you!).

A well-fitting harness to attach the long line to: By 'well-fitting' I mean something that is secure, isn't going to be escapable if the dog backs out of it, but that isn't rubbing underneath their armpits or restricting their shoulders. I also tend to use different harnesses for walking or if you just need to be able to handle your dog, e.g. to stop them running out of the front door! More on harnesses later, on page 69.

A drying coat: For use in the car after a wet, windy or snowy walk. A drying coat is usually made from towelling or a type of fleece, which will absorb the water and mud after a walk or run. The purpose is to keep your dog warm and wick the water away from their body during the car journey or walk home. These kinds of coats can be important for our puppies to make sure they aren't sitting in cold water or drenched fur that can over time impact the hips and joints. This isn't the same as a coat to use in the cold.

A bag to carry your toys and treats in: I tend to use a crossbody bag, like a bumbag. When you have a new puppy, these need to be going out with you on every single walk, so make sure your puppy bag is suitable to be carried on your shoulder or waist and doesn't take up valuable hand space, as you will need both hands when fiddling with your lead, puppy and treats! And make sure it is something you can easily wipe down or pop in the washing machine without too much effort.

For playing

Don't get carried away, as you need to meet your puppy first and suss them out a bit to understand what kind of toys they will interact with best. Also, don't forget, the world is your dog's playground – so a cardboard box or a single pea dropped on the ground is as incredible to your puppy as a shop-bought toy.

Rather than go out and buy fancy toys, I'd recommend:

A few cardboard boxes of different sizes and thickness.

Toilet roll or kitchen roll tubes.

Old tea towels or towels.

A variety of soft plush toys with tails and long limbs that are well made.

Flat toys that don't have stuffing in: These can be great as they are light enough for a puppy to carry and pick up and can be used in several different ways, such as tugging or rolling up with treats inside.

Treat toys: I love a KONG Ballistic hide 'n' treat ball toy for dogs of all ages and sizes. You hide treats in this Velcro toy and your puppy has fun finding them. (The KONG brand is better known for their rubber food-dispensing toys but, to be honest, I'm not a huge fan of these; I struggle to get things out of them, and I've got fingers!)

A sock stuffed with fabric and knotted at the end.

Tugger toys: Something you can hold onto one end of and the dog can hold onto the other and pull. Avoid hard ones like rubber as they aren't much fun for anyone. You can even make a tugger toy with the leg from an old pair of jeans – cut the leg into strips, then knot them all together.

Balls: At least three different ones so you can see what texture and weight your new puppy prefers. For example, a tennis ball, a squashy rubber one and a solid rubber one.

Treats and chews

A puppy is building its body with every meal and treat, so it's essential you give it the highest-quality food you can afford, even when it comes to treats. I recommend single-protein, high-quality treats such as chicken fillets and cod bites. Avoid items full of carbohydrates like wheat or soya. Cheap treats will be full of fillers, which will equal more poo for you to pick up, as the filler needs to come out because it isn't digested by the dog's body. What you put in counts!

I divide treats into three options, for different uses, as follows:

- The gold treat option: These treats are what I classify as high value. They tend to be smelly (super-interesting) and could be fresh meat, pieces of frankfurter, cheese, home-made liver cake. Use these high-value treats for rewarding in tricky environments and when trying to teach something when there are distractions around, e.g. recall around other dogs.
- The silver treat option: A treat that is interesting but won't make them go gaga. For example, dried liver. These are great for rewarding training you are actively doing on a regular basis.
- The bronze option: A fairly standard treat for rewarding everyday things like going for a wee outside or teaching them to stay close when walking on the lead. For example, a dried biscuit of some kind, cut-up veg or fruit.

The reason that chews are a necessity and not a nice-to-have is because of what they can 'do' for your puppy. Chewing is incredibly important to allow your puppy to calm, to be able to process experiences, soothe pain, relieve boredom and to allow exploration with their mouth. We can of course use vegetables like carrots or broccoli stems, but you do still need to offer natural animal-part chews as part of their repertoire. Such as:

Quick chews: I define a quick chew as one that will only last a few minutes, e.g. dried meat. You can dehydrate your own strips of meat in a low-heat oven over six hours, or it's much quicker if you have an air fryer.

Natural chews: By these I mean pizzle sticks, lamb ligaments, buffalo tripe sticks. Again, I advise you to choose chews that are a single ingredient when possible, and not heavily processed. Do make sure you avoid fatty things like pigs ears dipped in fat as anything with high fat content can aggravate tummies. Duck and pork tend to be higher-fat options than turkey and fish.

Raw meaty chews: Varying kinds for painful teething days. There are some great raw meaty bone guides out there – look at mypetnutritionist.com for one. If you are wanting to introduce them slowly, you can give chews that don't have any bones in but have raw meat and arrive frozen, such as trachea tubes. If you have a smaller dog, cut a tube into smaller chunks. Never give cooked or dehydrated bones as these can splinter. Raw marrow bones and oxtail are some of my favourite options to use once or twice a week. These are great for keeping teeth fresh and exhausting a puppy but do introduce these slowly so as not to upset stomachs.

What you really don't need to buy!

For feeding

Slow-feeder bowls: These are bowls with obstacles to eating, designed to make it harder for your dog to access their food. In theory this will help a dog who bolts their food. However, I'm really not a fan of these for dogs who eat quickly. If you need to slow them down there are many other methods you can use rather than frustrating them with these bowls. If you have a dog who is a resource guarder, definitely do not use these as they build frustration. If you do feel that your dog is gulping food and not chewing it, then you can look at changing the food you feed. It may be better to put them on a dehydrated option that you rehydrate, or a minced raw food that is less chunky so they won't choke on lumps. You can use a mixture of hand feeding with a bowl, it does just really depend on your puppy.

Expensive feeding stands for dogs for whom the floor may be a long way down: There's a simpler solution – just buy a plant pot of the height you want, fill it with soil, plant some grass in it and put the bowl in the middle! The pot will catch any remnants and the dog can eat the grass too. I did this with the water bowl for my Great Dane as it kept the flowers watered!

Liquid you add to water to stop plaque build-up on your puppy's teeth: These liquids are typically full of chemicals and, in my view, you should avoid them. Instead, use decent, fresh food, brush their teeth and give them fresh meaty chews which clean their teeth effectively.

Sleeping

Crates: These are one of my biggest bugbears. Your puppy does not require or 'have to have' a crate. If their breeder trained them with it and they genuinely enjoy it and want to use it, then definitely get one. If you are buying one because it's the 'done thing', you don't need to bother. It is worth remembering that the wide use of crates came from the USA where many trainers insist on dogs spending all their time in them unless they are toileting or being walked. Which makes me feel really sad when, actually, their time should be used to learn independence, to explore and learn to self-settle. If your dog adores the crate, then carry on as you were. Just don't feel like it is your only option.

Calming beds: Usually touted on social media, these are made of cheap fabrics with no support for your puppy's head or back. Many of my clients' dogs got overwhelmed with these beds and spent the entire time humping and trying to destroy them due to the texture of the man-made fabric.

For walking

The flexi lead: I'm not a huge fan of those extendable flexi leads, unless your dog is tiny and has zero pulling power. Otherwise I think they are dangerous, as they can get wrapped around people's legs, cut your hands if you need to grab the lead, and teach your puppy to pull. You definitely should not be using these on the streets where your dog can get away from you and end up under a car. Instead, use a 2m lead on the street and a 5m long line in the park. They can also be useful for dogs recovering from operations where you are building up exertion over time. Please never use them on bigger dogs with power behind them, they are not safe.

E-collars: Now illegal in several countries, an e-collar is a piece of equipment with a control held by the owner or trainer which emits an electronic shock via the collar. Trainers who use these will justify them by saying that if used correctly they are fine. This isn't an argument I can get on board with. Inflicting pain on purpose should not be part of our remit.

Prong collars: Most commonly used in the USA and often validated by people with big dogs. These are metal chain collars with prongs that face inwards into the dog's neck, so that when the dog pulls, the chain tightens and the prongs dig in, inflicting pain so it stops them from pulling. This still is not a reason to use such an item on your dog. I had a 65-kilo Great Dane, so I understand walking a large dog, and inflicting discomfort is not the way forward. No matter what anyone tells you.

Head collars: These are a piece of equipment that goes over the dog's mouth or muzzle area and usually fastens under the jaw to keep the dog under tight control. These would really be my last resort if, for example, you were very frail or poorly and couldn't walk your dog without it. Otherwise, they can, in my experience, create issues for the dog's muscular system in the neck and for the gait of your dog because of where you put all the pressure. I see many bigger dogs wearing these and, in some cases, it changes the way that they walk. They often end up looking like they are walking on tippy toes as they cannot walk in a full stride like their build is designed for, and this can create structural and muscular-pain issues for your puppy later on.

Harnesses that make your dog walk like a soldier: They do not allow for the full rotation of the dog's shoulder which is a big issue. Harnesses should not be too short in the body and sit right behind the legs, they should fit mid-way around the stomach, not right behind the front legs/armpits. Lastly, think very carefully before using over-the-head harnesses, as they can be scary and noisy for dogs and actually too heavy for many, with large clips clinking and different things attached. Look at where clunky heavy clips sit on your dog's body: would you like that?!

Dog coats: Most breeds do not require a dog coat. Unless you live in a cold climate or one where the temperature drops regularly, or you have a very short-fur dog breed like a Whippet or Italian Greyhound. Definitely do not buy any kind of coat with a hood, padded collars or which stop the shoulder movement of the dog when walking and running. (I really like some of the fleeces made by Equafleece. They are light, allow movement and wick away water and mud.)

For playing

Squeaky toys: I try to find toys without squeaks, as the sound can overstimulate some dogs and be annoying for others. If your dog is one that likes to demolish the toy to remove the squeak, then purchase to let this destruction work take place! You can even bulk-buy squeakers online and sew them into random bits of fabric or cushions for your dog to go to town on.

Hard rubber toys: The majority of puppies won't chew on these as they are too hard and too heavy. They might suit some bigger dogs but I'd still never use them and would prefer an antler or meaty bone for any dog, as chewing on plastic and rubber risks it being ingested. Natural is always a better option.

Snuffle mats: These fabric mats where you hide food for your puppy to find are fine but not required. They don't tend to occupy the dog for that long and, to be honest, you can wrap treats up in a towel, or throw them in some grass, and your dog will be just as happy seeking them out there.

Those laughing, giggling toys often advertised on social media: Not worth the money, and some dogs can be scared of them.

Treats and chews

Fake food: Avoid cheap treats filled with meat and animal derivatives – the lack of labelling means it could be anything, good or bad. Remember that words like 'natural' or 'farm' have no official meaning when it comes to dog food.

Treats where the first ingredient is wheat: Your puppy does not need this in their diet, it is a cheap filler.

Brightly coloured treats made with artificial colours.

Chews dipped in fat, e.g. pigs ears.

Cans full of treat sprays to fill toys with: These are full of chemicals, and I prefer to just use a cheese spread, sandwich filler or coconut oil instead.

Fatty chews: Some of these can cause upset stomachs, such as beef tendons. Touch and feel the treat before you give it to your puppy. If your hands are greasy, it's because they are dipped, coated or covered in something.

Cooked or dehydrated bones: These splinter in your dog's mouth and shards may end up in its stomach.

'Dental chews': These offer limited benefits for a puppy's teeth. Take a look at the ingredients – dental chews can be made from sugar, salt and artificial ingredients. Raw bones, vegetable chunks and animal parts are a much better way to keep your puppy's teeth in good condition.

Now that we have discussed your options of items to buy or not to buy, it's worth spending some time browsing online as many of the big chain pet shops don't sell the items I've mentioned. There are many brilliant independent brands, makers and creators who would love to chat to you about what you are looking for and help you out. And social media is excellent for second hand items, you just need to sterilise them properly before use – I love Nancy Birtwhistle's natural cleaning solutions, and she has all the recipes in her green-cleaning books.

PUPPY-PROOFING

The day has finally arrived! The day you may have been waiting your whole life for, so we want to make sure it goes smoothly and that you feel ready for it. Working on the assumption that you have researched and selected a brilliant breed, breeder or rehoming charity and puppy from the litter, this is what you now need to do.

Before you go and collect your puppy, you need to get your home set up for its arrival. The first part of this is puppy-proofing. I mean doing a proper job of going through your home to look for hazards, not simply tidying away a few shoes and hoping for the best! Here are some things you need to do to properly to puppy-proof your home, whatever size or breed you have chosen.

- Pick up and put away *anything* you do not want your dog to put its mouth around. This will be the case for the next six to nine months. Dogs don't care about the cost of the shoe, the expense of a handbag or the love you have for that limited-edition fabric ottoman. So if you don't want your puppy on it, chewing it, biting it and weeing on it, it needs to go out of reach – into storage if necessary.
- Electrical cables and wires that the puppy can reach need to be wrapped with cable protectors. These prevent the puppy from biting through wires and killing or electrocuting themselves.
- Install your puppy gates where necessary, e.g. to prevent them running and falling up or down the stairs; at the door to the hallway so that they can't reach the front door; etc.
- Set up your dog beds around the house. Supply more than may be needed, fold up blankets and pop them in random corners – you don't know where they are going to want to rest.
- Either remove rugs you care about or buy rugs you don't care about and put those down.
- Make sure that you have plenty of non-slip surfaces available for your puppy to access to lay on, sleep on and play on. If you have floorboards, lino or tiles, you must have rugs down for your puppy to use and to prevent joint issues later on. This is not a nice-to-have, it is a must to prevent big problems for your dog when it is older.
- If you have a garden and only want your puppy to access certain points, set this up before you pick the

puppy up, so the garden is ready and not a stressful situation later on. You can easily use bamboo sticks and chicken wire to fence off flower or vegetable beds or areas where you don't want your puppy to wee, chew or dig. You can set up a sandpit in the garden if you think your puppy may like to dig. Just make sure you have a lid so it doesn't fill with rainwater and to stop foxes using it as a toilet!

- Create a toy basket that your puppy has constant access to at any time. Establish another basket or drawer for items your puppy doesn't have free access to, which are only used for playing with you, for the park or for chewing. This makes the restricted toys a lot more exciting for your puppy.

- If you want to allow your puppy on the sofa, set up steps (you can purchase proper steps or make something with books) so you can teach your puppy to use them from day one. Same with your bed.

- If you live in a flat or have a balcony, set up your toilet-training area and make it a decent size. I've created them for clients in their bathrooms or balconies, but the key thing is, your puppy needs to be able to walk around the area – just one square of pee pad is not enough. And I strongly suggest you don't *just* use pee pads as you end up toilet-training twice. Instead, think about what you want your puppy to use when outside. For example, if living in a city it is handy to have a dog who will toilet on concrete, so set up paving slabs – even if you just buy ten of them and set them up in a corner, then put a pen around them to denote the toileting area. Choose an area and set it up properly, with space for the puppy to walk around, as toileting requires movement to stimulate the bowel and bladder.

- Do chat to your breeder or rehoming centre and ask for photos and videos to see the kind of set-up your puppy is using, so that you can try to mimic as much as possible. For example, if they are in a pen, if they are using grass to pee on, if they are sleeping on a memory-foam mattress – all of this intel is so incredibly important to know. Just as consistency enables all of us to do better, the same is true of the transition for puppies.
- Find out the food your breeder is using and buy enough to last you one week. Do not buy more than that. You do not want to invest in bulk-buying kilos of it as you are likely to want to change it after one week. More on that later, on page 194.
- Do send the puppy collar you are planning to put on your puppy to your breeder and ask them to start using it, so that when you pick your puppy up they are already used to having it on. Buy a small, thin puppy collar with a cat tag, so it isn't too heavy or clunky.

WORKING FROM HOME WITH A PUPPY

I think it is important to mention working from home with a puppy because, now more than ever, this is a common scenario. As we saw in the pandemic, working from home can allow people to get a puppy when they never thought it possible before.

But I have found that few people fully appreciate that bringing a puppy home is going to have a significant impact on the amount of work they can get done. You are going to be up and down like a yo-yo. You will need to be doing socialisation breaks, scenery changes, walks, training, loo breaks and more. You will not just be sat at your desk while a puppy sleeps calmly by your feet. Do refer to page 10 about taking two weeks off work, as this applies to WFH too!

I mention this as early as possible in the book – before you've even brought your puppy home – because I think it is important for you to be prepared or, if you are already living with your puppy, to remind you that the challenges of working with a puppy are all 'normal'. You are living with a baby animal who is eager, curious, wants to explore, has teething pain, gets tired, gets overstimulated, behaves like a land shark and like a furry teddy bear, all at different times!

When you are thinking about structuring your WFH day, be realistic and think about the timing of online meetings (is it a puppy sleeping time or a puppy feral time?). Look at the set-up of your room. Will you need a baby gate, a puppy pen, maybe a few sleeping options for your puppy?

It is common to think that, once we have walked a dog or puppy, we have given it enough stimulation for a few hours at least, but a puppy needs a lot of play and attention, not just for entertainment but for its socialisation and development. Of course we can offer a puppy independent activities, but when we are working from home we can fixate on giving lots of tasks that are solitary. These tasks have to be balanced out with interactive ones with you too. Lastly, carve out time every single day to give one-to-one interaction to your puppy. If you don't, your puppy is going to badger you and it will actually cause more chaos in the long run. Refer to your schedule or even write it out and factor in time for proper play. This is not sitting on your laptop holding a tugger toy, but time where you get on the floor to play and fully focus on your pup.

If you are going to have busy days where you are going to really struggle to give your puppy the time and mental stimulation it needs, then it is worth considering finding someone who can come into your house and do the things you can't. You can find a friend's teenage child that you can teach what to do, or a dog sitter who has time to come in for a few hours a day. This investment will pay off because you will be able to get proper work done, your puppy will bond with someone consistent, they will be receiving one-on-one care in their own home and you will be given details of what they did together while you were working. It will mean both you and your puppy are happy, rather than you just feeling frazzled and your puppy being feral as they aren't getting what they need.

Do think about factoring this into your schedule by finding someone before you bring your puppy home, and in terms of cost, as it will add to your puppy budget.

HOW TO BRING YOUR PUPPY HOME

This day is a special one, your phone camera roll is never going to be the same again!

Here is what you need to make sure you have with you to pick up your puppy from the breeder:

- A blanket or towel for them to sit on in the car/crate/lap.
- Pee pads to put underneath the towel in case of accidents, so they don't go on your lap or into the car or train seats.
- It could be worth looking at homeopathic remedies for car sickness to give your puppy before travelling, to make sure this doesn't become a 'thing' that then impacts your puppy later in life because of a poor experience on that first collection.
- A couple of options of where your puppy can be, according to how they feel comfortable travelling. For example, you might decide to have a travel crate set up, with you sat next to the puppy, and you might have a travel box set up and seatbelted in, in case they prefer that kind of set-up.
- Poo bags and wet wipes in case of any accidents.
- A bag to put in all the bits the breeder gives you – paperwork, blanket from mum and so on.
- It may sound strange, but you should ask the breeder if you can bring home with you a dirty pee pad from the puppy pen they have been using. Put it in a ziploc plastic bag and use it when you get back to

immediately rub around the toileting area you have created, to help transfer scent and help your puppy feel comfortable using the area.

- Bottle of water and a tiny bowl, as stress creates thirst – and your puppy will, however prepared and thoughtful you are, find this day stressful.
- Remember to bring home a blanket that the puppy has been sleeping on with its littermates. You can either send one in advance to bring home with you, or most breeders (and rescue centres) will already have this prepared.

One thing that many owners aren't prepared for is the removal of the puppy and taking it home. Seeing how hard this is for the puppy can be surprising for many owners, especially if you are taking children with you. Whether you are picking your puppy up in the car or travelling by train, the main aim is to minimise the stress your puppy will feel as much as possible. Removing your puppy from their lovely, cosy set-up is going to be hard enough for a dog that is only a few weeks old.

If you are taking kids with you to pick up the puppy, they do need to be fully briefed to leave the puppy alone and not over-handle, grab, shout and argue over it. Which I am fully aware is easier said than done, but you can do practice runs with a toy dog in the car and let them get the squabbles out of the way so that when the day comes they all fully know what to expect. Preparation and rehearsal with kids is key, as you can't expect them to know how to behave around the puppy if you haven't shown them, illustrated it, walked it through and played games around the idea. Just discussing it is not enough for children: they are not mini adults, they are kids!

If you are in the car, then I would make sure someone is sat with the puppy. They/you should sit in the back with the option of the travel crate, the box bed or your lap. This is certainly not a time to be removing contact from the puppy and expecting them to be OK on their own. If using a crate, I would advise that you put in a soft long toy for your puppy to be able to lean against, as they would against their littermates. Do not allow children to be fiddling with, overwhelming and handling the puppy here either. There will be plenty of time for interaction later. This is about keeping the puppy calm and reassured.

If you are travelling by train, look at taking a dog bag with you for your puppy to travel in. Do make sure that the bag you select is supportive, allows the puppy to remove themselves from interaction and snuggle down, and does not have their head hanging out so that people can touch and push themselves on your puppy. You can buy some great travel bags with mesh on the sides and with a roof that unzips so that while sat on the train you can have the bag on your lap and the top slightly open so that you can touch and reassure your puppy but other strangers cannot make contact. Do make sure that in the bag you have a soft toy for your puppy to lean on and against.

I'd always recommend that at least two of you go to collect the puppy, so that if you need to stop, get fuel or grab a coffee, one of you can remain with the puppy. Leaving the puppy alone – for the first time ever – in a strange, noisy environment will create stress that isn't needed for that first foray out of the safety of their nest and into the big wide world.

THE FIRST WEEK: YOUR DAY BY DAY GUIDE

Day One

So you have collected your puppy and arrived home safely. First mission accomplished: well done!

The next thing you want to consider is making your puppy's environment quite small and restricted so as to not overwhelm them.

When you first arrive inside the house from the trip home, I would immediately pop your puppy down in the area where you want them to toilet – in the garden, balcony or bathroom allocated area. You should have the area fenced off so that you can let puppy in and have them wander around. If they weed in the car or on the mat or towel, then rub that wee on the area you have set up – we want it to smell of them so that it signals that this is familiar and safe. If they don't go, it is fine, but you are going to take them back there every ten minutes until they do (unless they fall asleep). We really want to try to establish an area that is for toileting from the moment the puppy arrives home. As soon as they do eventually toilet, give gentle praise and a tiny little biscuit treat. Single bits of kibble work well for this kind of thing.

For the rest of the day, you are going to be taking your puppy out to the toileting area every fifteen minutes, or after ten minutes when you see them drink. Reward them each time they go to the loo, wee or poo. Don't pick up the pee pad or poo if they toilet in the allocated area. Leave it there to make the area smell of them until they get used to the idea.

Your day is going to be largely led by your puppy, so let them explore a little if they are up to it. This will of course depend on where you live, because if you are living in a small basement flat, exploration of that is pretty easy and possible, but if you are living on a country estate with outbuildings we will need to break that down into more doable chunks. If they want to retreat and sleep, you will leave them to it. They may hide somewhere like under a sofa. Do not try to bring them out, lure them or tempt them. They need time to decompress, to observe and to be allowed to figure out what on earth is going on. Don't allow kids or family to go and lay next to them. If they aren't seeking you out, it is because they don't want your contact. Harsh but true, and it is a good motto to live by with dogs.

If your puppy wants to explore beyond the area you have restricted, then just sit on the floor and let them get on with it. You can open doors to other rooms for them to go into. Because you have puppy-proofed, you are all set up and you don't need to trail after them. Please do not follow them into the room.

When your puppy chooses to explore, it is crucial you do not get up and follow them. And this is why it is so important that you puppy-proof properly. Knowing they can't get up to any damage, you can relax knowing that they cannot hurt themselves because you have done your prep work. We need to allow and cater for your puppy's independence from day one so that we do not create a dog who struggles with separation. If your dog is looking to wander off, let them. If they aren't, that is fine too. You can set up cameras in other rooms that you can view from your phone or tablet, so you can watch what they are doing but don't need to physically be there.

Be led entirely by your puppy on this first day. If they are picking stuff up and wanting to play, let them. If they are just chilling out and watching, let them. Be sure to go about your normal activities, e.g. cooking dinner, unloading the dishwasher, as you want to set the tone for the future. As tempting as it might be, don't simply sit and stare at the puppy as that is not what the rest of their life is going to look like!

If your puppy is following you, let them. Just don't reward the following by petting and talking to them as they do it. If they want to follow for reassurance, that is fine and I've no issue with it because you have just landed them in a new environment. But don't actively encourage it. The same is true when they go off and explore. Let them go, but do not then reward and react to them returning, or else you are degrading the exploration and elevating the return, which actually isn't right. Think of it this way: do you make a huge song and dance when your partner/kids/parents return from the loo or from another room? No, because it's no big deal. The same is true of our puppies.

If they have toileted in another room, it's fine, just go in and clean it up when they aren't with you. No big drama as you have puppy-proofed and removed precious rugs, etc.!

None of these things are big issues, so let them go and remember that you are on Day One of creating a puppy that you want to happily live with for the next ten to fifteen years.

Your puppy is going to be exhausted on Day One. They will either happily find a place to nap and get to it or they will fight it and go into exhaustion and that can look like over-excited behaviour. When our puppies are exhausted, it can actually look like they have energy. They may start jumping up, biting you, grabbing ankles, doing laps, but if they have been awake and it is close to their nap time, then this will indicate that you have left it a bit late for the nap, so they are now exhausted and don't know how to calm themselves down. Either way, with an eight-week-old puppy you need to remember that they should really only be awake for thirty to forty minutes at a time before they need to sleep. So making sure you are giving plenty of opportunities and setting up spaces that encourage rest are important.

If you feel like your puppy is on the over-excitement scale due to feeling anxious but not sure what to do with themselves, you just need to strip things back. Make sure you are not playing too much, do not wind them up, do not throw toys to fetch, but supply chewing items and provide a calm and quiet space. Even if that means you just sitting and watching the TV or working on your laptop and letting your puppy realise that it is quiet time.

For your first night, I would strongly recommend that you either have your puppy in your bedroom with you or you sleep on the sofa next to your puppy's pen or bed. You cannot expect your puppy to sleep alone after being removed from its litter. I'd also add that, generally speaking, unless you have a very independent puppy, most dogs want to be near their family – that isn't weird or dependent. Dogs are social creatures designed to bond. It is we humans who have created these strange narratives that they need to sleep alone and in a box. In reality, dogs and puppies need to sleep in a way that means all of you will get rest and that you are all happy with. I have a client who, on their first day of bringing their rescue puppy home, all got into bed together and that is where their dog has remained to this day. That is what they as a couple wanted and they have no plans to change this. Sharing a sleeping space doesn't mean you are screwing your dog up and that they will get separation distress. (My client's dog can happily be left home alone for a few hours.) Separation distress is far more complicated than just stemming from your sleeping arrangements!

For your first night, choose an option that feels comfortable and lets you go to bed feeling confident in your decision; if your puppy is a rescue, you can ask the foster carer what they were doing. I've had clients who have:

- Made a bed beside their bed with walls of cushions to keep their pup contained but comfy and cosy.
- Had their dog in their bed sleeping with them.
- Created a pen in the bedroom for the puppy to be in.
- Created a pen in the lounge and had it next to the sofa where they slept.
- Used a crate.
- Had a crate with the doors open within a closed pen.
- Had a bed option beside the sofa for puppy to sleep in.

- Had the puppy sleep at the end of the sofa, while they slept on the rest of the sofa.

What I'm trying to say is, there is no one size fits all – don't get caught up in believing that one way works for every dog and that your dog must only do one thing. Because what works for someone in a flat may be different from someone in a four-storey townhouse or someone who lives in a country house. Each puppy, each home, each set-up differs and that is fine. But in all of these scenarios, you would never let the puppy cry in distress without comforting and reassuring it. That is outdated advice and your puppy will need reassurance in this strange new place without the support of their mother and litter.

I tend to advise clients to be led by their puppy about getting up in the night to go to the toilet. If your puppy is moving around and disturbing you, then pick them up and carry them outside. Don't walk them or else they will pee or poo *en route*. If they stay asleep and don't disturb you for the loo, then happy days, enjoy your sleep! Remember, you will be right by your puppy, so you will hear them mew, squeak, move or nudge you. If your puppy is happy to sleep alone, you can always use a baby monitor for your peace of mind.

When you do get up, simply take them to the allocated area that you have already established that day. Let them go, reward them and put them back into their area to sleep. They may take some settling, so you may need to put your hand into their bed or keep it on them to let them know you are there and present.

Do expect that your puppy will be awake early, by which I mean around 5 a.m. That isn't strange or unusual. You are going to need to get ready to adjust your sleeping patterns for a while, as puppies don't really know about your desires in terms of sleep: they are working to their own little system! You would do best to get up at 5 a.m., have a little play, potter around, take them for toilet break and then try to get them to go back to sleep at 5.40 a.m. so you can get another hour or two, rather than trying to get them to settle at 5 a.m. – it usually won't work as they are fully charged and ready to go.

Our work on Day One needs to focus on creating bonds, building trust and nurturing a feeling of security and safety – that is where your priorities must lie. Don't worry what your friends did with their dog or what your grandpa tells you they used to do with their dogs, this is now and this is your dog.

Day Two

Hopefully you are waking up after an OK night's sleep – it won't have been your best but it should allow you to function! And if there are a few of you in the family, one of you can always take over while the other one gets a nap in.

You will need to structure your day based around your puppy's naps, e.g. awake for forty minutes then napping for an hour, on repeat throughout the entire day.

If your puppy feels pretty confident, explorative and into everything, then you can start to plan some little trips for each day. If your puppy is quieter and seems quite chilled, don't push it. Go at their pace.

For the confident pup, you can take a ride to a local retail park and sit in the boot of the car together and let them watch and observe people from a distance. You could sit on your front porch doorstep if you have one, with your puppy on a lead, and let them watch people walking on the road. You could carry them in the dog bag to go and pick up a coffee from your favourite cafe. You could set up different surfaces in the house or garden to try playing games on, to get them used to new feelings underfoot, e.g. laying out a piece of carpet, a piece of astroturf, a piece of cardboard and a long metal baking tray and gently placing some treats on them to encourage your puppy to go and walk on them, take the treats, have a nice time and not slip or have anything scary happen. Do this a few times for a five- to ten-minute play session, then pack it all away.

The idea isn't to overwhelm or overdo, it is to slowly and positively introduce – and to create a neutral or happy association with – different stimuli. This will mean your puppy isn't overwhelmed by different surfaces underfoot when going on its first walks with you.

I always say that you should be looking to do two to three outings per day. And by outings I do not mean big over-the-top things – see page 152 on socialisation for more information on this topic.

You can, of course, start to work on training some simple cues such as 'sit', but please, I beg of you, do not make training commands your priority this early on. Your focus needs to be building trust, understanding your dog's motivations (I talk about this a lot in my first book if you want more detail) and figuring out how to have a great time together. When you have that sorted, the rest can follow. If you put training before trust, you might have a dog who can sit and lay down and give paw but you won't really understand them, won't bond and you will feel frustrated with their behaviour because they aren't responding the way you want.

Always remember that you are dealing with a baby animal who is learning about the world. I want you to spend time showing them the world, building their confidence, reassuring them and playing together.

I suggest you keep a chart about your puppy's behaviour that the whole household will contribute to. This can be used later on for training, but also to make sure you aren't setting your dog up to fail by putting them in situations they dislike or are unsure of.

You just need a big piece of paper and on it you are going to draw boxes with the titles:

My puppy . . .	
Likes	
Isn't sure about	
Loves	
Doesn't like	
Is struggling with	

And you are going to start filling them in when you learn things about your puppy. So here would be an example one for Bramble, my client's rescue puppy:

My puppy . . .	Bramble
Likes	*pulling things apart, learning about toys, going out on walks, digging, chasing*
Isn't sure about	*people coming to the house, tugger toys*
Loves	*her owners, other dogs, treats, running around, bed, using her nose*
Doesn't like	*fluffy toys that move weirdly, balls (not a dislike, but she's not that bothered about them)*
Is struggling with	*focus outside, not wanting to take treats outside of the house*

And you are going to keep adding to it because you are learning about your puppy every hour, and we want everyone in the house to be on the same page. So if your dog isn't interested in chasing balls but one of you keeps trying to play with her in that way, you are going to find it harder to bond as she isn't interested and isn't motivated to play like that.

Starting this work early on gives you a head start as it also starts to show you where time should be allocated. For example, if your dog is unsure of people coming over but adores other dogs, you could start to arrange for friends with amazing dogs (calm, gentle, won't scare your pup) to come over so they could play in the garden. This will encourage your puppy to see that visitors are the gateway to play with other dogs. That is a very basic example which wouldn't be right for each puppy, but I just wanted to illustrate how you begin to utilise the information you find out from your behaviour chart.

Day Three

By now it should feel like your puppy is settling a bit, is happy to explore, is perhaps using the garden to snoop around in if you leave the back door open or sit outside with them. These are all really positive signs that your dog is starting to feel comfortable and understands that this is where they are now living.

Continue with your two or three little outings per day, varying what you are doing and when according to your lifestyle and set-up. Do bear in mind that your outings are not going to be full-on walks where the puppy just saunters next to you! Your puppy is going to stop, sit down and need time to just watch, so more on that within the socialisation section on page 152.

For me personally, even at eight weeks old, I do still take tiny puppies out on one walk per day and put them down on the pavement to walk. It depends where you live and the environment you have access to will slightly impact this, but in my opinion we need to be teaching our puppies what we want them to do in outdoor settings immediately, not waiting until they've had their final jabs at twelve weeks.

You may be slightly panicking and wondering why I would recommend putting your puppy down on the ground if they haven't yet had their second vaccination. Let me reassure you that many vets agree that, because the majority of dogs these days have had primary inoculations, diseases like distemper are now thankfully rare.[*] The risk of your puppy not being properly socialised to outdoor life in its first weeks, and all of the noises and sights it will have to get used to, are in my opinion (and that of many vets) of higher importance to your dog than the risk of contracting a rare disease. As long as your puppy is healthy, carefully introducing it to other healthy dogs is better in the long run than keeping it solitary for too long.

It is of course your decision as to what you do with your own puppy, but I did want you to have this information too when it comes to walking puppies outside in their first weeks at home. We as owners have to make decisions based on our home, our dog and our life. No one, not even a dog behaviourist, can go back in time and

---

[*] www.londonvetclinic.co.uk/our-services/annual-health-checks-vaccinations/our-dog-vaccination-policies/

change the impact of a poorly socialised puppy, and for some dogs (like poor Pudding) this poor socialisation can be the foundation of many of their behavioural issues as an adult. Lack of socialisation is the reason we are putting so many dogs down per year in the UK and USA due to their behaviour rather than illness.

I'd suggest that on one day you go for a short street walk around where you live, provided the area is relatively clean and not full of other dogs. I'd only do this for around fifteen minutes and on the lead. If your dog stops, let them sit and observe. This is their way of letting you know that they need more time to figure things out and learn about the environment. If they want to come home, let them come home. You are simply showing them where they live, what is around them and that there is an outside world while they are in an early socialisation period (eight to twelve weeks-ish). Never push your puppy, force them or make them, each interaction has to be led by your dog. Even just walking around your driveway, if you have one, is an outing.

Do think about when you are meeting people and don't allow each and every person to say hi or get involved in coming up to your puppy. The world can be an overwhelming place, so be cautious and make sure it is an interaction your puppy wants, and not just one that they are putting up with because they have no choice. Otherwise this can bring issues in later life where your dog actively reacts to people as they want to keep them at bay.

For the other outing I'd either carry or drive the puppy to a park, field or relative's garden and put them on a harness and 5m lead to let them explore while you sit down with a cup of tea! The aim isn't to walk them far, it is to introduce them to the idea of being out of the house in a place with smells, and what you want them to do in that situation. You will sit with treats in your pocket and any time your puppy looks at you, comes over, turns around and glances at you, you will either throw them a treat or give it to them. You will not call them over or lure them. This is giving them the time to learn that what pays off is re-engaging with you, interacting with you and looking at you. A very simple but hugely, hugely powerful lesson for your puppy. Again, choose an area that is quiet, where you can sit relatively undisturbed.

At home, you will still need to be taking your dog out to the loo every fifteen minutes and sleeping with your dog. This will go on for quite some time, so don't expect there to be a quick fix. But by Day Three you might be starting to see little signs that your dog uses the allocated toilet area immediately and is actively trying to access it or reach it of their own accord. Hooray if that is true!

By Day Three, I would be starting to allocate times where your dog cannot access you, not in a mean or stressful way but more in the sense that you are busy doing something so your puppy needs to entertain itself. You cannot and should not be entertaining them 24/7. Your puppy needs to be allowed to go off and find their own amusement, to come across items you have left out and to explore. You might do this by simply sitting on the sofa and working on your laptop, or reading to your child or watching some TV, so you are present but not interacting, playing or providing activities. But do make sure you have set up things to amuse your puppy or else they will just find their own things to do that you may not appreciate!

You can set up what I call 'exploration floors', which is where you actively create a floor covered in things for your puppy to learn about, teethe on and chew and all of it will be safe because you have selected the items to put down. This is great for tiring a puppy out, but, much more than that, it is amazing for learning about textures, smells, new items and preventing resource guarding.

An exploration floor can be as complicated or easy as you have the time for. It could be placing a huge tablecloth on the floor and hiding treats in its folds and then allowing your puppy to walk all over it, move it around and play. Or it could be made more complicated by putting out lots of objects from around the house, such as boxes and loo rolls from the recycling bin, which you let your dog bite, chew and pull apart. The key is that by doing an exploration floor, an outing and a walk each day, you start to build up your puppy's resilience, interests and desires – and you are a part of them.

Your Night Three should be starting to feel predictable, in that your puppy knows the format, is reassured that you are close by and will start to have an idea of when, if at all, they will want to get up to go to the toilet.

Day Four

Your days are going to feel like Groundhog Day by now, I can't lie about that! But each week, as your puppy grows, their abilities will develop, including their ability to stay awake for longer. In this first week, I would make the most of having a puppy who can only be awake for such short time periods as this will change very soon.

By Day Four, you should be factoring in times to work or to sit at your desk (or wherever it is you work from), so that your puppy starts to get used to your set-up. Initially you should try to coincide these times with naps or when your puppy is getting tired, but you will soon realise this isn't always possible and you are going to have times when you need to complete something while your puppy is being feral. In these situations, you will need to get your dog to calm down and the best way to do that is to use sniffing or chewing options. That might involve filling an empty box with shredded paper and hiding treats underneath it all, refilling as you go, or letting them have a chew in their bed while you complete your work or task.

You might be beginning to think about the kind of play that you want to do with your puppy and whether you are creating habits that you want to continue for the rest of the dog's life. For example, if your puppy is a Whippet and you are only playing chase games with them, it could be annoying later on as you have a breed already designed to chase and you are reinforcing that drive every time you play. Instead, with a Whippet, I'd be looking at rolling a ball and asking your puppy to wait until you release it to collect. Focusing on creating a *wait/release* will be way more helpful with a puppy bred to chase. The same with playing tugger: it can be ace for teething puppies and for interactive play, but if it overstimulates your puppy, and leads to biting and nipping, then you need to start looking at differing toys, different textures and different ways to play so that you don't keep pushing your puppy into a way of play that means they can't focus, listen or learn because they are so hyped up.

It is worth mentioning that when people have puppies it can be really easy to just start lobbing a ball to wear them out, but I ask you to start this with great caution. Ball lobbing can create huge issues later on in life if we create a fixation or if we have a dog with an obsessive nature, as we can inadvertently create a problem. Teaching a 'fetch' game in theory is OK and something that many dogs will enjoy, but there is a difference between a dog who enjoys fetch and a dog that will only play this game and nothing else. It should also be factored in that the process of chasing a ball repeatedly with fast, frantic stops can cause long-term injuries that we really want to avoid, and so you should think about how you play this type of game. For example, it is far better to be rolling the ball, not doing lots of stop/start, and if you are going to throw the ball, aiming for it to land in long grass. This is so that the dog isn't doing twists, turns and slipping over as, I promise you, it will damage your dog's structure, muscular system and growth plates, which can end up costing you financially but also emotionally if your dog ends up lame, needing surgery or permanently damaged.

You can also start to teach your puppy their name, in a really easy and fun way. Taking tiny treats, you are going to put one on the floor and let them scoff it. As soon as they finish, say their name – they are going to look up at you anyway, because they finished the food you put down and will hope for more. So you are going to simply pair that reaction with their name and build on it. Do about twenty repetitions for each little training time and within a couple of days your puppy will be able to respond by turning round or looking up when they hear their name.

Do remember that your puppy's name is not their recall cue, so you will need a different cue for calling your puppy back to you. Their name is simply how they know you are talking to them, so try not to use it to ask them to come to you. They just need to look up when you say it and you can then wave, give a treat, throw a toy, etc.

If your puppy is struggling with their confidence, now that they have begun to settle at home is a good time to start thinking about incorporating some confidence-building games. These are games that are easy wins for your puppy, which build up their confidence and create a bond with you. Here are a couple of examples that you could start with:

- Lay down shallow bowls of different sizes and materials on the floor (e.g. a metal bowl, a ceramic bowl). Walk between the bowls, dropping treats into them for your puppy to sniff out. This should be super easy but also allows for each bowl to feel and sound different as the treat hits it. Once your puppy gets into the game and begins to happily move between each bowl, you can start to space them out a bit. This encourages more movement and more sniffing around which is always good for releasing stress and anxiety. If your puppy is even unsure about putting their head into a bowl, then instead use something shallower, such as a few baking trays or flat plates.

- Create a very basic but fun agility course in your hallway using everyday objects. For instance, lay a broom flat and a coat on the floor and use treats to teach your puppy to walk over them to see that nothing scary happens when they encounter an unfamiliar item in an unexpected place.
- Sit outside on your front step and watch the world go by from a distance. Don't allow people to pet your puppy if the puppy is anxious and shrinking away. Instead, let your pup sit and observe. Keep the front door open so they can retreat inside when they need to. We just want to offer opportunities for your puppy to learn about new people, objects and noises in a calm, controlled and non-confrontational situation.

By Day Four, you should be allowing your puppy to venture further in its exploration of the house. If you are happy for your puppy to go upstairs, then you could be starting to teach them how to use the steps. Do this by placing a tiny treat on each step so that the puppy learns to take each step at a time, slowly. Don't encourage them to race up the stairs, and at this stage always carry them down the stairs to avoid damage to joints, growth plates and ligaments in the puppy's developing body.

If they are allowed upstairs, you can start to do things like have a bath or shower and leave the door open to see if your puppy has the independence to go off and explore, or whether they stay with you the entire time. If they do stay with you, allow it, but don't chat to them or reward the behaviour. If they go off and explore, again it is fine as you will have puppy-proofed or shut doors to rooms you don't want them in.

Day Five

If your puppy has really enjoyed their time out of the house, it could be a good day to arrange to visit or meet a friend with a dog that you think is a great role model for your puppy. By this I mean one that isn't too boisterous or rowdy, and one who won't react aggressively to your puppy. This will allow you to start teaching your puppy how good interactions with other dogs work.

Do not just let both dogs tear off, running and playing with each other for an hour. Instead, I would suggest meeting outside the house with both dogs on the lead. Do some parallel walking, side-by-side, using treats to keep your puppy's attention on you rather than the other dog (this will be hard work!). Then if you or your friend have a private garden, head there and let the puppy and dog have a brief play (ten minutes) while interrupting the play every two minutes to get them to disconnect from each other, and come to you to receive a treat. Both dogs should get a treat so they're both equally motivated to stop playing! After ten minutes, I would lure your puppy away, again using treats, and the same with your friend and their puppy/dog, and then put them both on the lead and try sitting down for a cup of tea while you reward both with a chew on the floor next to your seat. This will be teaching them about calm time as well as how to chill out and leave each other alone. The whole thing should really only last about thirty minutes in total. Keep it brief and be realistic about what you can expect, but also focus on what you want your dog to be like around other dogs when they are older, as you are setting the scene now.

When you pass or see other dogs in the street, do not take your dog over to them. Instead reward your puppy with treats for walking past. This is really important as you do not want your dog approaching and walking into every dog they see, so we begin to teach that as early as possible, in their very first interactions.

Make sure you are encouraging great habits around the front door at this stage too. When the doorbell rings, don't allow them to go with you to the front door. Leave them in another room like the kitchen and if no one is coming in, then they never get to see the person at the door. This just means that we avoid friction (e.g. your dog barking at the door, running at the door, defending the door due to fear) around the front door later on, as it won't be something your dog has paid much attention to.

Eye contact is the key to connection with your dog throughout its life, and we want to instil the habit in your puppy of checking in on you regularly (and you will do the same for your dog). Beginning to establish this connection between you very early is key.

The simplest way to do so is this simple exercise:

- Sit on the floor holding a packet of treats (nothing too exciting or smelly).
- Put your hand in the packet so your puppy can't put their nose in.

- Let them try to paw you, nibble and jump on you to get the treats. Just ignore this.
- As soon as they look up and give you eye contact, mark the action with the word 'yes' and reward them from the bag immediately.
- Repeat this twenty times and then put the bag away.

Play this game every day for two or three minutes each day. You can then start to do the same exercise with toys and with their food bowl, so that they begin to learn that eye contact is everything. I truly believe that if we focused on teaching our puppies this, we would have much happier dogs, as they would learn from week one that when they want something, are scared of something or are unsure of something, they just need to look at you and make eye contact and you will respond by rewarding, getting them out or creating an exit plan. That is what a relationship looks like.

Day Six

If your puppy is a breed that will need regular grooming, you can start teaching some grooming etiquette in a very simple way. Place a textured rubber mat on the ground, spread with something like peanut butter. While your puppy licks the mat, you gently brush them, using something very soft like a baby brush. When they stop licking, you stop brushing. You only need to do this for a few minutes per day but it's a really nice way to introduce it early on and each day you can brush a different area of the puppy. If your puppy pulls away and walks off, it means they aren't keen, so leave it for the day, tidy up the mat and restart tomorrow.

On Day Six you can also begin to teach a 'touch' cue, which has so many uses later on. Simply hold a palm outstretched and hide a treat under your thumb pressed to your palm. Put your open palm in front of your dog and let them boop it with their nose, trying to get the treat – when they do this, immediately release the treat. Repeat with the other hand until you can get your puppy moving between two hands. You do not call or say anything, you simply use your hand as the symbol that you want them to reach out and make contact. This was actually my deaf dog Cookie's recall cue and she would run over to me as soon as she saw it. It is also an excellent game to play when your puppy is getting tired and a bit feisty and you need to rein it in a bit and calm them down. You can play this touch game to bring them back into a calm state, then move them onto a chewing item and try to get them to settle down for a nap.

If you have a workspace outside of the home where you hope your puppy will accompany you in the future, you could use today to take them there for thirty minutes. Take them at a quiet time so they can have a calm wander, learn about the office, perhaps see a couple of people who will be chilled with the puppy and then head home. Don't overdo it. Remember that you are setting the scene for future dates so if you let your puppy run riot, jump on people and be wildly overstimulated, this behaviour is likely to be repeated the next time you visit as that is their association with this new place. So really think about picking a time and moment of the day that will be beneficial for you and your puppy.

Day Seven

By now, you should be starting to carve out a bit of a routine for your days. You'll be better at knowing when your puppy struggles, when they tend to be calmer, and recognising their indicators that they need the loo. And the annoying thing is that next week it is going to change all over again! But don't be panicked, as you and your puppy will have already learned so much about each other. While each new week and month brings challenges and changes, it is also hugely rewarding to see your puppy develop and learn.

Day Seven is a good day to have a visitor such as family or a friend. Begin the introduction to your home with a short visit. Try to let your puppy get to know this person or people, show them the touch game or name game and let them play it, and start to build bonds and associations in a good way. Let the person or people come out on a short walk with you. Let them hold the lead and show them how you are doing things, such as interactions with other dogs. This is about helping your puppy understand this is someone they will be spending time with and they are a great person to hang around with. I wouldn't advise letting kids hold the lead and do this exercise as they can end up creating some issues with timing of giving treats, running with puppies dragging them and so on.

You should be starting to think about the week to come and planning ahead, too. Know that with each week your puppy grows, so will their needs. To set yourself and your puppy up for success, you should be actively planning your days, thinking where you will go and what you will do, which toys you may rotate in their toy basket, things you have struggled with this week and how can you make it easier for you both this week. For example, if your puppy is struggling to settle and nap in the day, think about rejigging bed areas, factoring in disconnection times where you work and puppy sleeps, and taking them in the car for a nap when you go to get a coffee. Life with a puppy is never perfect or simple, but you can make it easier by having realistic expectations as I hope I've set out here.

A tired, overstimulated puppy will be your worst nightmare. They will bite, nip, jump up and chase, and it will feel full on. So sleeping and naps need to be a focus for all puppies. Moving into your second week (of likely a nine-week-old puppy), they may now be able to be awake for forty-five to fifty minutes at a time, depending on the breed and their size.

I would also get ahead on making or filling up mats and treat-dispensing toys, plus ordering your chews, as their teething and biting is about to kick off and you want to be prepared. You can even make and freeze them to get ahead.

On this day, you could start to do some off-lead work, or drop the long line when in the park. You could do some walking next to each other and reward your puppy for being where you want them to be, near you, with little treat pieces. Once again, think about what you want in the future and start training for that, knowing they won't be able to do it all but trying to show them how to do a little bit, and building on it.

Be realistic in this first week – aim for two minutes of walking next to you off-lead with treats and then release them by throwing a treat into the grass and saying 'off you go'. Have two minutes of free sniffing time and then resume the training of walking next to you. Puppies have short attention spans, so don't make it boring and don't make it too long.

So your first week with a new puppy is over! Congratulate yourself, as in your first week you have:

- Worked on allowing and encouraging independence.
- Started work on confidence-building games.
- Begun to teach your puppy its name, the touch cue, off-lead manners, how to interact with a dog, walking beside you and more.
- Taught them about the immediate world around where they live in a gentle way.
- Started on the incredible foundation of eye contact.
- Introduced the idea that touching and grooming contact is nothing scary.
- Allowed exploration of surfaces, fabrics, objects and encouraged discovery with their mouth.
- Provided time to observe, learn and watch the world and its inhabitants.
- Given them the opportunity to meet a dog that means good things.
- Introduced them to another caregiver who will be a positive influence and part of their life.

That is a gigantic number of things for one week! And all of them are so important for helping your puppy become the dog you want to live with for many years ahead.

THE PUPPY BLUES

If you really feel like you are struggling, not enjoying your puppy, can't bond with it or are finding that everything feels too much for you, you may have the Puppy Blues. These are very real and very valid feelings, and should not be ignored or swept under the carpet. Your life has changed in a significant way and it is entirely normal to feel confused and overwhelmed. Here is what I would suggest you do if you are having any of these feelings right now:

- If you have struggled with your mental health previously and feel that the puppy could have triggered something, please speak to your therapist or a mental-health professional immediately. Don't wait and don't delay it in the hope it will disappear. Recognising this and talking about it is a huge step, but one that could really benefit you and the puppy. Please don't feel bad, scared or ashamed. We all come from differing backgrounds and experiences and when we take responsibility for a puppy, it may bring up many emotions. I've worked with clients who have found their puppy triggered feelings of vulnerability that they did not feel able to cope with. You are not alone and, if you have one, your therapist is best placed to help as they already know you, so email or call them that day.
- If you are struggling to bond with your puppy, then think about how you can make your life with your puppy simpler. Stop thinking about what you 'should'

be doing. Stop worrying about schedules and how you should be raising your puppy and simply do things that help you enjoy and see the goodness in your puppy. Perhaps that is driving to a new park together and just sitting with your puppy on their long line while they explore and you sip a coffee. Make life simpler, not harder, for you and your puppy.

- If you are finding it overwhelming, then ask for help. Ask your best friend, your parents or your neighbour if they can dog-sit so you can go to the gym or out for a puppy-free walk for a break. Just be consistent with who you ask, as you really don't want to pass a puppy around to lots of different people. But don't be afraid to say 'I need some help'.

- If it is early days and you genuinely feel that you have made the wrong decision, contact your breeder immediately. It's better to ask to take your puppy back at eight weeks than at sixteen weeks. At eight to ten weeks, the puppy can still go to a new home during its socialisation period and be able to settle well without a lasting impact. The longer you leave it to give up your puppy, the harder you make it for the puppy's future. So try to not think of yourself and put the puppy first in this situation. Any decent breeder will have asked you to sign a contract to say that they will take the puppy back in these circum-stances. Please do not use social media or third-party sales sites to advertise the puppy. This is not the fair, responsible or right thing to do. And if your breeder won't help you, you can speak to your vet and hand over your puppy into their care.

CHAPTER THREE

Your Puppy's Developmental Milestones Explained

The thing to bear in mind about our sweet dogs is that their developmental milestones are different from ours. This is because their lifespans are so much shorter than ours, and that means their key development moments can come thick and fast in those early months. It can be hard to keep up! If you are already living with your puppy, this fact will have started playing on your mind by now.

So let's go through some of these key developmental milestones to flag some of the most common issues I see at these stages. I've divided this section broadly into blocks of three or four months per stage, but do bear in mind that all puppies are different and these timings will not be exact. Our dogs come in such a huge variety of shapes and sizes, and their development is also not one-size-fits-all. In my experience as a dog behaviourist, I've found that many of the bigger breeds can take longer to mature and can have an extended 'silly period', as I call it. Every dog goes through a period of not listening, losing their mind a bit, forgetting all the commands they've learned. I've realised over the years that breeds like Labradors, Vizslas, German Short-haired Pointers and Golden Retrievers can often experience this for longer than other breeds and I put it down to their size. Because they're big, they look physically mature, but their brain and emotions haven't quite caught up!

So please don't get too caught up in the phases, or think your puppy is either very mature or very immature based on the timelines below. Instead, I'd encourage you to use these broad time periods as guidelines while knowing your dog may differ and this isn't anything to worry about.

MONTHS 0−2

During this time, your puppy will of course have been born and be living with their litter, hopefully being raised in a wonderful way. This is the timeframe when your puppy is being imprinted on and learning about their world week on week. It is why it is so important that your breeder, rescue centre or foster carer is super-involved and proactive, because during this time they are responsible for helping to set up our puppies to be resilient, confident, non-confrontational, happy little dumplings that will be a great addition to your home.

Where your puppy comes from and these early experiences are so important. Your breeder or rescue centre might have a webcam you can access to see daily goings-on, to watch the puppy muddle through life, and to see what they are up to. Each week as they develop and grow they will be understanding more, and you will see tiny differences week on week. The breeder will give them their first vaccinations for you to continue when you get them home, in week eight and week twelve of life. Even during these early days we can start to see personality traits and differences between the puppies, and it is these things that are you are looking for when you visit to choose your puppy.

Our puppies in this phase will be trying different foods, mum will be spending less time with them and they should be being exposed to new experiences in a kind and carefully considered way, such as different toys, different surfaces, exploration of the home, sounds, touch, vet visits, car journeys, play in the garden if the weather suits. There is so much an active, caring breeder should be doing to ensure that the puppy you take home is set up beautifully for the next phase of their life. In the UK, most rescue centres should be doing the same; if you are looking abroad, it's worth doing extra research into specific rescue centres' environments.

This period of the puppy's life is often described as their 'primary socialisation' as it is when they are with their mother and litter.

MONTHS 2–6

Ideally, your puppy should have arrived with you by eight weeks of age. This is because we want them to be landing in your home, and your set-up with your family, in this key phase when they are at an inquisitive and curious period in their development. These early weeks are crucial for socialisation for your puppy, and I would always advise getting a puppy at this age if you can. (Some breeders will try to hold on to their puppies until ten weeks, but I prefer to get a new puppy in your home by nine weeks of age at the very latest as this window is small. Bear in mind that if you live in a busy city there is a lot going on to get your puppy acclimatised to.)

In addition to getting used to their new environment, I believe that we want to be using this time for your puppy to bond with you and your family, and this formative time is crucial for that relationship-building.

During this four-month window of time your puppy will go through several 'moments' and those will likely be: their secondary socialisation period, a fear period and then what I call the 'lull into a false sense of security' period. Let me explain!

Secondary socialisation

The secondary socialisation period is not an exact set of weeks but we tend to say that this stage occurs from between eight to thirteen weeks (roughly). This is a period where your puppy is excited, wants to explore, to learn and be curious, to touch and feel everything, mouth and figure out what their new world is all about. So providing them with slow, small, positive experiences is really key to their development and confidence, and will be super important in forming how they will view going into adulthood.

I often see adult dogs who have been deeply impacted by how their socialisation was handled and so I can't deny that this time is important. Our puppies are growing and absorbing the world around them, and building up or breaking down their resilience, their trust, their feeling of security and more. Which is why I really want the puppy home with you in those weeks, so that you are in control of what is going on, as it's highly likely a breeder's life will be different from yours.

During this period it is all about small, gentle and considerate experiences. It isn't about going everywhere and doing everything. Read in more detail on page 152 about socialisation and how to do it well.

Fear period

After this secondary socialisation period, at around fourteen to sixteen weeks of age, I often see puppies go into what is called a 'fear period'. You may start to see things like your puppy not wanting to leave the front garden, or doing part of the walk and then wanting to return home, or needing to sit when out and about and just watch, and, very often, not wanting to walk at all. These actions are all 'normal' and to be expected. The puppy is working out, rightly, that not everything in its new world is safe. And this is a good thing as, while we want a confident dog, we don't want an overconfident one with no boundaries.

This is a very sensitive time for a puppy, and if we try to rush through it the impact will show up later on, as they won't have been given the time to figure out the scary world around them and to form neutral feelings about different experiences. Dragging your puppy when it wants to sit, forcing it into interactions it doesn't want – these can all form patterns of fear which stick.

Understand that your puppy is stopping simply because it is temporarily overwhelmed. In these situations, I advise that you let your puppy take the time it needs. If you need to get somewhere in a hurry, then carry your puppy or put them in a bag so they can watch and learn without feeling overwhelmed. Where you can, though, just let them sit and observe from a distance; it is a truly powerful experience for your puppy. To you it may look like all they are doing is watching or sitting, but in fact they are taking in scents and hearing noises we may not detect, as well as observing. If you remember from the first-week guide earlier, I mention sitting on your doorstep and observing from the boot of the car, and these are all perfect tasks for during this time. The outside world can be a sensory overload that we cannot fathom. Just because you can't see it, smell it or hear it doesn't mean it isn't going on for your puppy.

False sense of security phase

Next you will go into the 'false sense of security phase', which is often a really delightful period when your puppy has learned lots of commands and is responding brilliantly and being such fun to hang out with. At this stage I've seen a lot of owners feel very confident that all their hard work and dedication is paying off. And it is! But there is a lot more development to come, including an often-challenging period of regression, so I would suggest you enjoy this phase while keeping in the back of your mind that it is going to end! All puppies must go on to the next part of their journey.

Teething

During this period, teething is going to kick off! You'll find a whole section on this process in the next chapter (page 132). However, it has to be mentioned in these months because it will ramp up and then start to die down, depending on your puppy's experience – again, no dog goes through it at an exact time. Fundamentally, teething has to take place for our puppies to start to cut teeth (when their teeth cut through their gums), use them, explore the world and use their mouth. There will be days or times of day that are worse than others, there will be times where they manage to nip your nose, grab your clothes, attack your feet as you are walking across the kitchen, and it can be really hard to not take it personally. But – and it is a big but – there are many reasons as to why and how our puppies use their teeth, because it isn't all just about tooth pain.

What you need to think about for your puppy's developing body

When your dog is born, they have growth plates at the end of their bones/limbs and these plates are responsible for the growth and development of that bone. These growth plates are much softer when puppies are born and have a higher chance of fracture or breaking – which is why it is so important to be aware of them and the impact you are putting on them. We want to make sure:

- There is healthy and proper growth of each bone and limb.
- That growth plates are not damaged.
- That bones are not restricted in their growth and completion due to damage of the plates.

What we need to make sure of is that in our everyday life with our puppies we are not placing unnecessary pressure on them, not allowing them to risk damage and not exercising them in a way that could mess up their growth plates for ever.

The tricky thing for owners is that I cannot give you a set date when growth plates will be closed and complete. For smaller dogs this tends to happen earlier, e.g. at one year, but for our bigger breeds we could be looking at between one to two years. There is no certainty without having your dog sedated and scanned, which I wouldn't advise as we want to give as little analgesic in our dogs' lives as possible.

So here are some ways to make sure you are protecting your puppies, their bones and growth plates:

- Rugs, rugs and more rugs.
- Do not let your dog slip, lose grip or chase things on floors without rugs or carpet.
- Restrict jumping, make sure they land off a sofa onto a rug.

- Avoid other dogs pummelling them in the park – this can have a big impact.
- Don't let them jump out of cars.
- Be extra cautious around chase games, running into things and too much exertion.
- Consider the impact of dog day care if you use it.

EXERCISE AND AGE RESTRICTIONS:
THE FIVE-MINUTE-PER-MONTH RULE AND WHY
I DON'T USE IT

We have to factor in the exercise we do and what we are giving our dogs access to that can impact their health and growth. Many people have used the idea of five minutes' exercise per month old a puppy is. So, if your puppy was five months old, by the guidelines of this theory you would exercise your puppy for twenty-five minutes per day. Which is just insanity to me and many of the practitioners I work alongside!

If you were only exercising your puppy for twenty-five minutes per day at the age of five months, you would be pulling your hair out, your home would be trashed, your dog would be feral and you would very much be regretting your decision to take on a puppy.

So here is what I suggest to my clients instead. Let's focus more on what you are doing with them and make sure we aren't risking their long-term health while also ensuring we help your puppy socialise, learn and become the dog you want to live with. Otherwise restricting their outings from the house this much will have grave consequences for the emotional development of your puppy.

AN EXAMPLE OF A DAILY EXERCISE PLAN FOR
A TWELVE-WEEK-OLD PUPPY:

Morning: Fifteen- to twenty-minute walk, with no destination in mind. This could be around the block, just on your street, or you could drive to a park and take them out (carried in a bag and then put down somewhere). This would be low-level, low-impact walk, so there's no risk to the joints. I call this a 'potter' walk. You don't actually need to be 'walking' for that duration, but you will be out and experiencing the world.

Lunchtime: Scenery change – hanging out in the front garden, with the gate shut, or sitting in the back of the car in a shopping-centre car park, watching everyone go past. Sit on a bench together watching the world go by.

Afternoon: Fifteen- to twenty-five-minute outing – on grass, a softer surface, which could be a friend's garden you drive to, a park nearby, wherever you can let them off to explore and reward their contact with you. Or it might be a vet visit and potter around the car park or a trip to a pet store to sniff about.

Interspersed with this, you would also have free play in the garden if you have one, play with you, plus mental stimulation, chewing, training, etc.

Even as our puppies get older and reach twelve months old, it can be tempting to think about running with them or letting them run while you cycle or the kids scoot. Again, we really want to avoid this as we don't know when your individual dog's growth will be finished. The risks to their discomfort, adding pain and creating issues later on in life, aren't worth it so it's best to wait another year.

If your dog loves playing with other dogs, you do need to think about the surface they are doing it on and, most importantly, the way they are playing. Each breed can play differently, so what we don't want is a puppy being constantly overpowered, pushed around, knocked over, run into and walloped by fast-moving dogs. You really will need to be your dog's advocate for this one and risk upsetting other owners, because they won't be the one paying for the medication later on in life when your dog develops issues from the damage done to their hips at a young age.

The idea is not that you wrap your dog in cotton wool, but that you are aware and make choices appropriate for your dog. Every puppy needs to be socialised, out and about, learning, playing, meeting, greeting and interacting. Restricting this would be damaging to their emotional and behavioural wellbeing.

Different breeds and their growth

The range of growth, weight and size varies from breed to breed and between genders, so it is impossible to give you a one-size-fits-all scenario here.

In order to support our dog's full development, we need to factor in a few things:

- The type of exercise and where we walk them.
- The bed they sleep in and the support it provides.
- The play you create, offer and allow.
- The surfaces your dog is playing on, living on and walking on in the home.

- The nutrition and diet you are supplying.
- The equipment you use to walk your dog, e.g. harness, collar and lead.
- Rest days (factored in for all ages of puppies through to senior dogs).

What is important to understand is that your dog's brain development, skeletal development and emotional development will all vary. They don't all just stop on the same day when, magically, your puppy has become a dog. It is a gradual process that your breed, their genetics, training, environment and food can all play a role in – so even if you and your sibling each have a puppy from the same litter, how they develop, mature and grow will still differ. This growth is another reason why I hold the views I do regarding spaying and neutering – more on that on page 127.

MONTHS 6–9

Temporary regression

When your puppy is six to seven months old, you may still be in the 'false sense of security phase', where your dog is listening in the park, leaving other dogs alone and is right by your side. This is amazing and exactly what we are aiming for. So it can be a big shock when your lovely, focused puppy suddenly starts finding all of these things very difficult. It may start to not listen, run off, not respond and seek out more independence, especially in the park.

It is a bit like an adolescent who understands what you're saying but realises that they don't actually have to do what you tell them! The puppy is testing boundaries as part of its development, and this is all perfectly normal. We want to remember that underneath this behaviour they are still our lovable puppies, but hormones and growth are starting to be involved and that can cause complications.

You may start to find that some walks go terribly, while others will still be OK. You may also notice that your dog is getting more interested in what other dogs are doing. So this is where the work really begins and will carry on for quite some time. For many dogs this isn't a short-lived phase, I'm sorry to say!

This phase is where we start to look at how we can continue to teach our puppies, while also not allowing them to reinforce behaviours we don't want in the long run, such as seeing a dog and bolting off after it. We don't want to dampen the spirit of our puppies, but we do need to be aware of this phase and start taking action, setting them up to succeed rather than just hoping for the best or doing what we have always done and then wondering why it isn't working.

During this phase you will really need to make sure you are considering where you walk your dog. We should be varying where we walk our puppy during this phase, and trying to factor in more spacious, quieter places so that our puppy isn't constantly being bombarded by a million things that will overwhelm them and make their behaviour more erratic. This can be difficult in cities, where owners find a decent park and repeatedly take their puppy there as it is local. But if the park is always full of other dogs, then you are going to struggle and every walk will feel hard. You can also try varying the timing of your walks to less busy periods.

As your dog's recall is going to be all over the place in this phase, I suggest using a harness and long line and lots of reward systems such as exciting treats and toys to encourage your dog to stick with you on a walk instead of running off. Also consider who (apart from you) is walking your dog to ensure that they are also briefed on the behaviour we want to reinforce in this stage.

Playing with other dogs

During this stage it is often tempting to put your dog into day care or with a group dog walker, but I'd still advise against it at this point. If you do need to, I would suggest that it is just for one to two days per week, absolute maximum, and that you have really thought about who it is. Do refer to page 270 on dog walkers and day care for more information.

The reason that we need to be aware of our puppy around other dogs is because they are impressionable, they are distracted, they are going to go a bit more feral and not listen as much. We want to make sure we aren't just letting them run wild and do what they want, or reinforcing behaviours we don't want. We of course want them to have some pals, but these should be well thought out meetings, parallel walks or supervised playtimes – not simply tearing after any dog and wrestling it to the ground!

Our puppies will come out of this phase, but it can last several months and be quite frustrating for an owner. There can be a temptation to just let the dog 'get on with it' and enjoy itself in the park, but this will cause you double the work later on. It may feel like the dog isn't taking anything in at this stage, yet it's a key moment when your gentle reinforcement and play will be sinking in at some level. When they come out of this stage you want to have an adult dog with solid behavioural foundations, and this will take time and patience.

During these months we would start to expect most bitches to have a first season. We cannot predict when this will be, so do not think about spaying your bitch during this time. Our male dogs will also begin to go through hormonal changes and may start cocking their leg or being more scent driven and wanting to mark everywhere. This is to be expected as they want to spread their scent further. You will also likely see and feel (!) your dog humping your leg, visitors and toys. This does not mean that they need to be neutered. This is actually a displacement activity, where your puppy feels overwhelmed or unsure and they are trying to calm themselves down.

MONTHS 9–12

The tricky phase

You're probably thinking – *haven't we just been through the tricky phase? I thought she said it was going to get better!* This is a different kind of tricky as, in my experience, your puppy will have grown bigger and look older, almost like an adult dog, but they still need a great deal of understanding and patience.

This time can be highly sensitive, and I believe that some dogs can have another fear period around ten to fourteen months, when slight changes in their environment or routine can really impact them. For example, a client of mine took their ten-month-old Pointer puppy camping. Initially he loved it as he got to sleep in the tent with all the family and was in heaven. One night there was a bit of a kerfuffle outside the tent and the owners thought nothing of it. But on returning home, the only place their puppy wanted to sleep was with its owners, whereas previously he had happily slept elsewhere. So we set about continuing to make him feel safe and secure while also slowly rebuilding his confidence, as it had taken a bit of a hit during the camping trip. None of this was anyone's fault, but it is important to highlight. I believe if you know about this phase you can plan for it. For instance, I would suggest that this phase is not a great time to book a big family holiday trip and leave your dog with a new sitter. Nor is it the right time to enrol them in day care, because things could go terribly wrong. Our puppies are little learning sponges and we need to make sure they can handle and thrive in the situations we are putting them into. The wrong set-up, dogs or people can do the exact opposite and can create issues within days.

This phase is one where we need to reassure our puppies and reinforce their routine to maintain their confidence. Know that this phase won't last for ever but, rather like in tiny puppyhood, we want them to come out of it unscathed and happy.

We may start to see our puppies becoming more un-certain around dogs in the park, or acting like they don't want contact from strangers. These things all tie in together. Don't force them into situations or interactions that they don't want. During this phase, don't do what you have always done just because it's what you used to do. Your puppy is showing you through their behaviour that some-thing doesn't feel right, and it's your responsibility as an owner to respond to this. During this phase your puppy will need more space to learn, it will want more time to watch, and it won't want to be hassled, so allow this. Responding to their needs will bring them out of this phase faster, and flourishing, because you gave them the space and quiet they were desperate for.

I think of it as a bit like how human teenagers go through that awkward phase where they can barely bring themselves to speak let alone look enthused or inspired about anything. I think this is the dog version of that. We just need to ride it out while providing outlets, boundaries, guidance and reassurance. During this time you may invest in renting secure dog fields to let your puppy off lead because you know they are struggling with listening, so that you can work on teaching them the cues and ability to listen but without panicking that they can escape or run off. It goes back to my motto of 'setting up to succeed'.

Breed traits emerge

Lastly, this time frame is when we start to see 'breed traits' come to the fore. So your Dachshund may find their voice, your Rottweiler may start to become more territorial around visitors entering the home, and so on. Knowing this can be helpful, as it means you can start to plan accordingly and be able to teach your puppy how you would like them to react instead of getting annoyed when they do. You might start teaching your Rottie puppy early on that visitors to the home bring gifts, so that their association with visitors is that they always mean really great things.

MONTHS 12–15

The hard work is paying off

Now our puppies will be starting to reach their full growth, though that doesn't mean that all their development is complete. During these months, you should be starting to see glimpses that the puppy who was listening and responding to you and being quite reliable is returning. It should be starting to feel like you can predict their responses and abilities more accurately as they gain a bit more steadiness and maturity. It won't be fully there, but you may start to see bits and pieces!

This isn't true of all the breeds, as you may have a bigger breed who is still gallivanting around the park, jumping up at everyone in a bid to lick their face. Don't despair, your time will come.

Spaying/neutering

Around this time we may start to think about spaying and neutering, but this will depend on your dog, their breed, size, personality and temperament. I would not think about neutering or spaying before this point because we want the dog's growth plates to be closed. We want to make a decision that is right for the individual dog and, for me, doing it at six to twelve months is too young. Ideally we would be looking at more like eighteen to twenty-four months, but there are many factors to consider. These include the dog density of where you live, your dog's confidence, your dog's reaction to people and other dogs. All of these are important to understand before making a decision.

MONTHS 15–18

Depending on your breed and size, you will feel one of these two things during this phase:

- Your puppy has reached maturity and it feels pretty solid. The last eighteen months of work have paid off and you are seeing the dog your puppy has become.
- Your puppy has another six to twelve months before they're fully mature, and you need to continue to keep your head down with reassuring, reinforcing, rewarding, and knowing that it will pay off.

Some of our dogs will mature at more like two to three years old, so please don't always assume a dog's maturity is just about the training someone has done. Each puppy's journey differs and there isn't anything that we can do in order to speed that up. Nor should we try to race through this phase, as I promise you that when your dog reaches their senior years you will look back and wish for some of that zest for life and silliness. So appreciate it for what it is now and if you are finding it hard going, make it easier on yourself. Here is how I recommend doing that:

- Walk in quieter places with fewer distractions so your dog can respond to you and you can capture the behaviours you like and desire.
- Alternate your walking days – do one day of big sniffy proper walks where your dog can be a dog enjoying everything in its environment, and then the next day do more training-style walks. You can't physically be 'on' all the time and nor can your dog.
- Factor in large chunks of time for mental stimulation and games at home that will tire them out, build a bond and reinforce habits you are working on like giving eye contact.
- Go to places where you and your dog can sit and observe at a distance and then come home.
- Rent a secure field so you can take a coffee and let your dog gallivant and get rid of some energy without you worrying about it running off, or its interactions with other dogs.

Your dog is your dog, so developing their life, routine and habits is what it is all about as they will be living with you for the next ten to seventeen years.

And if you are considering a dog walker or day care, I'd only really start to think about this from around twenty-four months onwards, depending on the puppy. More on that later. The only other reason I'd consider doing this earlier is if your rescue puppy really needs other dogs around to help them build their confidence.

By the time you've worked with your puppy through these developmental stages, it's tempting to feel like your work is done. On the outside, your puppy will develop pretty quickly and look like they are 'complete'. However, it is so incredibly important to remember that on the inside there is still a lot going on, a lot developing and we have to factor that in or else we risk causing physical damage that could have lasting effects.

When will they be an adult?

I tend to feel that a puppy is an adult when they are between eighteen months and two years old. If you have a smaller breed (e.g. a Dachshund), we might be more likely to see this at around eighteen months. If we were looking at a Hungarian Vizsla, then I'd be looking at two to three years minimum.

The important thing to consider is: what is their behaviour showing you? Are they silly, finding it hard to concentrate, testing boundaries, etc.? Or do you feel like they have come out of puppyhood and you are on an even keel?

One of my clients has a Golden Retriever puppy who is nine months old. He is 32 kilos already, his head is big and he looks like a full adult dog. Except when I play with him, greet him, chat to him, take him to the park, I can very clearly see he is most definitely not an adult dog. How? Well, here are some of the ways I can tell:

- I can only describe his walk and motions as like a crab, because he is so wiggly waggly, so excitable and bendy when he moves around.
- He goes into the world so curiously still, he is so desperate to learn, wants to watch and observe, to enquire, run off and find out.
- He's all floppy and, when tired, he can't keep going.
- He thinks everything and everyone is for him, as why wouldn't it be?
- He is learning control but we have days where it totally goes out of the window.
- He is starting to cock his leg but not all the time, just now and then.

None of these are scientific but they are behavioural, there for me to notice and advise his owners that we are still very much in puppy phase. So when they are expecting perfect long-lead walking, being able to stand in a coffee shop undistracted and to be able to walk him without chasing a leaf, I can tell them we are a while away from that!

We have to be realistic and this is important as it means

we don't set unrealistic goals for a puppy that isn't an adult yet. We don't expect things of them that we still need to spend months teaching, reinforcing, reminding and doing.

CHAPTER FOUR

Your Puppy Head to Tail

TEETH

Your puppy is going to go through a couple of teething phases, and that means chewing, biting and an appetite for destruction. We cannot swerve these phases, and the severity of them will depend on your puppy's breed, its mother, the litter it was raised with, their breed genetics and your environment. Just like children, some dogs teethe and suffer more than other dogs. The key to the teething phases is to be prepared and know that it is coming, and it is likely to be painful and exhausting for you and the family as well as the puppy!

If your puppy grows up with a mother who lets them know when they have gone too far with play-biting, then they will already have become accustomed to boundaries around using their teeth. If your puppy grew up with a great breeder who supplied heaps of different items, toys, chews, bones, objects to explore, mouth, teethe and lick, then you stand a great chance of having a puppy who knows where to direct their chewing because they had so much available to them. This is why breeding matters, as it is all in the detail.

I find that teething can start from seven and a half weeks; at this stage a puppy bite often feels cute and playful rather than painful. But by ten weeks the biting can ramp up and start to hurt and by twelve weeks it is agony if a puppy bites you, as its baby teeth are like sharp little needles. At this stage your puppy may be nipping you on the nose, the cheek, grabbing clothes, getting your toes and sinking their teeth into your ankles.

It's important to remember that your puppy isn't setting out to hurt you or anyone else with these bites. It relieves their pain to chew and bite, as they are transitioning from their baby teeth to adult teeth. As the adult teeth are popping out at differing rates, they will be causing different amounts of pain.

I think it is really important for you to also understand that teething is not the only reason your puppy is going to use their mouth on you. There are lots of other reasons, so here are my top five questions (in no particular order) for you to ask yourself when a puppy is biting you:

- Does it want to be left alone? Perhaps you are fiddling with them, touching them, stroking them, trying to pick them up and they don't want to be handled. Every dog has their boundaries.
- Does it have too much energy? If it's not been exercised or played with, then that energy has to go somewhere and can easily tip over into frustration.
- Is the puppy tired or overstimulated and struggling to calm down? Judging this can be hard, as it is

a very thin line between energy and overtiredness. Remember how much a puppy needs to sleep, and work out whether this could be exhaustion.

- Are they in pain? When your puppy's teeth are painful, they need to try and relieve the pain by biting and chewing.
- Could there be dietary deficiencies? These can become apparent when a dog or puppy starts to chew on things and actually eat them, for example sticks, mud and stones.

I think it is really important to point out that every puppy, and even adult dogs, requires chewing and mouthing activities on a daily basis. Younger dogs may need more chewing opportunities, but even senior dogs will need chewing to be a priority. Chewing on healthy items you have provided, such as a raw bone, or a fish cube, gives our dogs a way to wind down, relieve stress, pain and boredom, and enrich their life. When we look at feeding something like a raw meaty hip bone, it isn't just about the nutritional value of eating the meat off the bone but also about the physical manipulation that the mouth, teeth, shoulders and front legs need to do. It is about the constant use of the mouth, the ripping, the pulling, the shredding, the licking – all of these are incredible outlets for a dog of any age and this is why chewing activities are so important not only for dental health and hygiene, but for emotional regulation too.

I would go so far as to say that chewing is like Prozac for your dog! The more it chews, the calmer it will be. So don't neglect this opportunity to give your puppy a way to regulate itself. My only caveat is that some working breeds, when overtired, may need chewing *and* to be in a pen or crate so that they can switch off.

There are now heaps of 'chews' on the market, some of which are great and some are not. Here are a few items I'd suggest and some I'd steer clear of.

Chews I like

Dried jerky: So easy to make at home if you have an air fryer with a dehydrator mode. A jerky is made of just protein – such as strips of chicken or lamb – and the dehydrating process makes the meat harder so it takes little puppies time to chew them down. Mostly suitable for very young or tiny-sized puppies as they will be scoffed instantly by bigger puppies.

Pizzle sticks: If you don't know, these are a dried bull penis, which is grim but for many dogs they make a great chew as they are longer lasting. They do have an awful smell, which your dog will love, but you will need to have a window or door open or put them in the garden with the pizzle.

Dried fish cubes: A few of these are great for young or tiny puppies as they have hard edges for them to really crunch down on.

Naturally dried ears: Such as rabbit ears for smaller dogs or puppies, and cow ears for bigger puppies. Avoid any that are greasy to touch or are a dark brown or red colour as that is due to being dipped in fat and can cause horrible stomach upsets.

Raw meaty bones: Such as split marrow bones, hip joint bones and lamb's tail or oxtail as these have lots of meat on with minimal bone through the middle. Do not give cooked bones as they can splinter and cause injuries to your dog (including internally if they swallow the splintered bone). Be very wary of the bones in vacuum-packed-style packets: I would avoid these too as, due to the packaging process, they may be more likely to splinter, which can cause damage internally.

Household objects: Like cardboard boxes, tea towels, pieces of hosepipe, as their teeth can sink through the material. In addition, these can be carried around easily, don't stain or smell.

Himalayan yak chews: These are solid chews made out of yak's milk. They can be a good option for a puppy who really is a strong chewer or who wants to 'work' on something for a while. Once they have finished using it, put it away until the next time they need it. You do need to be cautious with making sure you buy the right size to prevent your puppy trying to swallow the whole yak bar or damaging their teeth on these, but buy bigger ones if you are not sure. Once finished, when there is just a stub left, you can zap it in the microwave and it will puff into a cheesy, crunchy treat for your dog to consume.

Chews I'm less keen on

Antler chews: I think most antler chews are not of interest to most dogs as the majority find them too hard, and they don't smell interesting enough. If you do want to try them, make sure you buy a split one as that is better for your dog's teeth.

Pigs' ears: A pig's ear can be OK for dogs, but many are now dipped in fat and are really greasy, so may cause an upset stomach, particularly in puppies. Check how the ear is preserved, as fatty additives can really aggravate your dog's gut. If they are dark brown or a reddish colour, it's likely they have been dipped in a fat solution. Please note, manufacturers don't have to list the fat it is dipped in as an ingredient on the bag or box.

Rawhide: These are the white- or brown-coloured chews in the shapes of bones, candy canes, etc. They are heavily processed with chemicals to make the skin bend and go into strange shapes, and for this reason I would advise against dogs digesting them. I am seeing more of these as plaited items not listed as rawhide, but that's still what they are. So if they are white and listed as made from skin, it is probably the same thing.

Cooked bones: These are often sold vacuum packed. You do not want to be giving cooked bones as chews even if you have cooked them yourself, due to the risk of splintering.

When you are living with a puppy who chews, I think it is important to point out that they can have a couple of chewing phases. The first is the early stage of puppyhood when teeth are being cut and they are learning about the world. The second is around seven to ten months, when we think they have grown out of it but they start reverting to the chewing and biting. Don't despair: this is normal, testing but expected. Your puppy is having hormonal shifts, becoming more curious about the world and being more independent. With this development comes a need to process, calm themselves and most of all to chew on items.

So don't worry about the chewing returning: you should expect this to happen. It just means that you will need to go back to factoring in chewing times and objects. Do note, there is a difference between an older puppy displaying some chewing behaviour and an older puppy who is chewing, mouthing, jumping up and grabbing everything. The latter behaviour would indicate to me that your puppy is struggling in some way, and there may be a larger issue to address. Do not simply ignore this behaviour and do not keep telling them off for it, as there is a reason why it is happening that in my experience will require a deeper dive. Always remember their behaviour is your indicator that something isn't right, isn't working or they are struggling.

One thing that will help you massively with teething is to be prepared. And by that I mean before you go to bed each night you should line up your puppy's chewing items on the worktop, stock the freezer or defrost items in the fridge so that you know you have three to six items ready to rock for the next day. These items can of course differ each day, but the overarching thing is that they last differing amounts of time – you want a mix of long-lasting chews and less long lasting, because if your dog is tired and needs to wind down, you don't want to be giving them a raw meaty bone that could take them one and a half to two hours. Whereas if your dog had energy and you needed to crack on with some work, giving them that raw meaty bone that takes two hours would be absolutely ideal. So your timing and your allocation of items is key. Do bear in mind that some dogs can find higher-value items overwhelming, so they may try to hide or dig the bone into mud. Most dogs will return to it a few days later! If your puppy does this, it could be worth playing around with smaller items first, e.g. dried chicken and duck feet, and then slowly moving on to raw duck necks that can be eaten there and then, and after a few of those, on to something else. Build them up slowly and introduce things at their pace.

When your puppy is going through a chewing phase, I would strongly recommend you put a baby gate or two up, so that if your puppy is really struggling or you have a day where you are misunderstanding your dog's cues (i.e. you misread their tiredness for energy) then you can get yourself behind the baby gate and avoid any biting of your nose, nipping at your ankles or grabbing of your toes. You can sit behind the baby gate and simply toss some cold chunks of cucumber or apple or frozen banana at your puppy through the bars until their frenzy has subsided and you feel OK to enter the room again. We all need management strategies in our lives, and for teething puppies a baby gate is absolutely paramount.

Children can really whip a puppy up and then find it upsetting when the overstimulated puppy starts to nip and bite. We cannot expect our puppies to contain themselves, hold themselves back and not react if we are not supplying them with the space they need, the chews they require and the calm space to settle and relax. This is one of the reasons I would always say to anyone with young children (aged eight or under) to really think about if bringing an overexcited biting and nipping puppy into your home is going to create peace and goodwill, or turn your kitchen into a fraught zone where everyone is crying (including, often, you!).

This is particularly true if you have children in the home with special needs or SEN requirements. My daughter has Autism and Sensory Processing Disorder and it is one of the reasons we have not had a puppy since she was born. The combination of her age and sensory-seeking processes means a biting puppy is not something she would be able to deal with all that well. And her needs would not be fair to a puppy either. So if you are considering bringing in a puppy or looking for an assistance dog for your SEN child, it is not as simple as *any puppy will do*, because the majority of puppies are not cut out for that kind of work and interaction. We have to think about the puppy's needs as well as the child's, and I've witnessed it go terribly wrong when parents purchase a puppy with no understanding of any of these processes, breed needs and child struggles. Bringing a puppy into a home with an SEN child needs to be a very carefully thought-out process, and to give you the best chance of success you will need help and bespoke guidance from someone like a dog behaviourist or a registered charity.

Finally, it's crucial to understand that your dog's teething needs are strongly related to their input (sleep, being well rested, using their mouth) and their output (getting rid of energy, stimulation, using their brain). Something that is really important to get a firm handle on is providing enough sleep to make sure your puppy is not exhausted and grumpy, and so is biting and teething on you because they literally are beside themself with tiredness. (Do refer back to my sleep guidelines on page 55.)

EARS AND EYES

Your dog's ears and eyes are a really good indicator of their overall health. A healthy dog's eyes are clear. They are not runny, have no discharge and are not itchy. The same is true of their ears. I have found that a problem with your dog's ears is often the first indicator that your dog is experiencing a health issue. Most commonly that will be shown through itchy ears, ears that have discharge, ears that smell, repeated ear infections, and you'll also see your dog exhibit behaviour like rubbing around the head and ears.

It's easy to think about our dogs' organs, limbs and body parts as all being separate, but I work in a way where we look at the dog as the whole picture (even though this section is divided into body parts, we still consider the whole dog!). If your dog has an issue with its eyes or ears, of course you should first treat the symptom with something like eye or ear drops. But if it returns, then don't just treat the symptom again, but instead consider whether your dog is suffering from an allergy, a gastro issue or something isn't working right in terms of what you are feeding, e.g. a protein allergy.

For instance, one of my clients had a dog who always had weepy eyes. She treated this with eye drops from the vet but it kept recurring. It took her, and her vet, a long time to recognise that this symptom was not an eye problem but an allergic reaction. When the vet recommended cutting chicken (a common allergen) out of the dog's diet, the weepy eyes stopped within a few weeks.

I'm seeing more and more cases of seemingly innocuous issues that began in puppyhood becoming worse in an adult dog. Vets often treat the symptom rather than the underlying cause, which simply suppresses the issue, so the next time it arises it comes back worse. Ear infections are a great example of this, because they can seem easy to treat. But let's say you start treating them with ear drops. The next time it is antibiotics; the next time it is antibiotics and ear drops; then it's a longer course of antibiotics and by six months of age your puppy has had their gut health wiped out from three courses of antibiotics in such a short space of time. Yet we haven't actually spent any time figuring out why your puppy's ears are presenting an issue in the first place. This is where bigger problems begin that get carried into your dog's adult life and then impact their behaviour as well as their health.

If you find yourself in a situation like this, you should try to seek out a holistic vet as soon as possible. You really want to be working with a vet who can see the whole picture and isn't simply medicating.

I am currently working with a young Doodle mix whose owners are at their wits' end and one of them is contemplating rehoming the dog. This is because he is struggling with his allergies so much that it is deeply impacting his behaviour. His previous vet simply dosed him up on monthly allergy injections and now we are in a situation where he has a compromised immune system due to this but we still don't know what the allergies causing the problems are. It is up to us to do the deep diving and it is a big part of my role with my clients in uncovering what is going on and what we need to do. So if any of this resonates with you, or you feel you are just starting on this pathway, now is the time to take action. The key thing to take away is that what you feed impacts your dog gigantically and if we do not figure out what is causing the issue but keep giving medication instead, the analogy of pouring water on the fire to put it out while pouring petrol with the other hand is a great description. You just won't get anywhere.

SKIN

There are many common reasons for skin rashes. As with the eye and ear issues above, it is really important to remember that whatever the rash, you should always get to the bottom of why it is there. Avoid just treating it with steroid cream, which again suppresses the issue without addressing the fundamental reason for it being there.

Some of the most common reasons for skin rashes, in no particular order, include:

- Dietary – what you are feeding is not working for your puppy. This could be as simple as removing a certain protein, or more complicated, which involves removing a few foods. Either way, avoid just buying the food recommended in the vet surgery, as that will not get to the bottom of what is causing the rash or inflammation. Go away and consult a nutritionist before choosing a new food.
- Inflammation – due to stress, trauma *in utero*, food, environment triggers, illness and so on. Do not underestimate how inflammation can spread into a much bigger problem if it keeps being supressed by medication.
- Flea bites that cause a reaction. (Even one bite can trigger it.)

You should be asking your vet for skin scrapes and swab tests, and if the rash continues you should consider seeking help from a specialist canine nutritionist.

When you are looking at skin-related rashes, hot spots, fur coming away and constant itchiness, it is incredibly important to remember (and this sounds obvious) that the skin is highlighting what is going on inside the body. I think we have become very disconnected from our own and our dog's bodies and see each organ as individual. But if an organ is struggling it will impact other organs and outputs. So once again, you need to seek out a holistic vet who understands this.

PAWS

This may also sound obvious, but your dog's four paws are precious things! They are the way your dog touches the world around them and we do need to be aware of the impact surfaces can have on our puppies. It may be your dog's first experience of sand or walking on a metal bridge, and so surfaces under the paws matter to your dog. It is why you will see your dog going crazy on the beach on the sand, digging at wet mud, jumping at waves and gallivanting through long grass. The texture and touch of a surface can be stimulating, exciting or scary for a dog, hence their reaction and interaction with it will differ from dog to dog. But being aware of this means you can also keep a close eye out in puppyhood, as if the sand sends them gaga you can factor this in and reduce your expectations of what they are capable of when at the beach, e.g. you might put them on a long line as you know they won't be able to listen, respond to you or pay attention when you first get there. Knowledge is power, remember! It is really important during your puppy's socialisation period that you introduce differing surfaces and create confidence around them. More on that under socialisation (see page 152).

It is also important to understand that your dog's paws need to be maintained and looked after as there are a few things in that area that can cause problems, either indicating something we need to be aware of or creating an issue themselves. Let me give you some examples:

- Dew claws. This is the nail/claw that is higher up on your dog's paw, at the back. It is a bit of a breeding throwback, as these nails don't really serve a purpose any more. But we do need to maintain the dew claws by keeping them short, or they can be ripped off during exploration and exercise. So teaching your puppy nail maintenance is really important from a young age. This can be as simple as helping them accept you touching their feet and between their toes, to them meeting a kind groomer and getting accustomed to what the process will involve. This is best done a few times during their primary and secondary socialisation period, so is worth checking with your breeder regarding what they may have done with your puppy before you take them home.

- Fur tufts. If your dog has fur that grows quite long, you need to be keeping an eye on the underside of their paws. Fur growing longer and out between the digits and main pad can cause your puppy to slide around, not be able to grip the ground or floor and can in turn create hip, knee and leg issues. Your groomer will trim their paw pads underneath and around the feet each time you take them in. So if you have a dog whose fur grows quickly or is long, you should book regular grooming sessions, even if each one isn't a full groom.

- Salt on the road. If in the winter you walk on streets where salt has been laid down to counteract ice, you will need to rinse your dog's paws after each walk. Salt can aggravate the skin and be ingested if your dog is licking to clean them.

- Digit licking. If your puppy is chewing at their paws,

licking them or pulling at them, it may indicate that your puppy has an allergic reaction that you need to investigate. Read more in the allergies section of this book (see page 209).

TAIL

Your puppy's tail is a rudder (used when swimming), a behavioural indicator (the way it wags or moves), an anchor (provides balance) and a way to spread scent (when meeting other dogs), yet we don't really pay too much attention to it other than thinking a waggy tail means a happy dog (not always the case!).

A dog's tail is an extremely important part of their body which helps us and other dogs read their posture, body language, feelings and more. There are of course varying types of tails, but here are some things you need to know about your dog's tail:

• Short or stubby tails (e.g. on Boston Terriers, English Bulldogs) can be problematic for other dogs as they either don't move or don't move very much, which means it can be hard for other dogs to gauge information. If your dog has a stubby tail, or no tail at all, you should be aware that this kind of tail conformation can cause sensitivity to the spine, as the lack of tail can sometimes impact the spine itself. We have to recognise that the conformation of our dog's body can and will impact their health and behaviour. So just because something is an 'accepted' part of a breed doesn't mean to say it won't cause complications for you and your dog later on. So do give these elements some thought.

- Longer tails will waft scent, without your dog even thinking about it. Dogs will do low-level wagging when another dog greets them, to move their scent for the other dog to take in and learn about it.

- Dogs cannot 'control' their tail like many people think. So a dog's tail will wag and move, even if going into a scrap or confrontation. A wagging tail doesn't always indicate happiness.

- There are different ways that your puppy's tail will move which can indicate how they feel, e.g. the helicopter tail wag, which goes round in a circle, tends to be reserved for people your puppy really adores.

- A tick-tock tail (where it moves slowly from side to side) can indicate uncertainty and can happen before a fight or scrap starts. This kind of tail is often seen as a standard interested posture in some of the bull breeds, which can then lead to misinterpretation with other dogs. For example, the English Bull Terrier's tail tends to move like this even when excited.

- The tucked-down tail between their legs is a posture seen regularly with dogs like Whippets as part of their body shape. However, for many dogs it is a sign that your puppy is unsure, anxious and isn't keen on an interaction. So if you are seeing this tail action around people, other dogs or kids, then you need to be cautious how you proceed and not allow your puppy to keep being put in situations that they dislike.

A NOTE ON GROOMERS

Whether your puppy is going to need grooming every eight weeks (in the case of non-shedding dogs such as Schnauzers) or once a year, it is important that in their eight- to twelve-week-old socialisation period you introduce your puppy to the groomer you would like to work with.

When you are looking to find a groomer, please do not just go for the business nearest to you. I would always recommend finding a small, local groomer who knows the community and its dogs. I trained as a groomer in the early days and used to offer a service where I visited clients at their homes, to groom their dogs who had been injured, distressed or upset by the groomers they had originally gone to. Many were scarred for life due to their early trauma with being tied up by the waist and neck, restrained, unable to move and forced into having grooming done to them.

What is important to understand about taking your dog to the groomers is that it can be enjoyable if you find someone who genuinely cares, is interested and wants to not rush the puppy through the process.

We need to take into account your breed of puppy, as some breeds can be more touch-sensitive than other breeds. For example, a Shiba Inu can be incredibly tricky to groom as they can be so sensitive to being touched. I once saw a puppy tied by the neck and bottom onto a table, screaming and screaming. The groomer was telling the puppy off and the owner was standing outside laughing as if it were funny that the puppy was that distressed and upset. It was heartbreaking to see, as that kind of trauma will stay for ever and impact their interactions with all humans, not just groomers. And then we wonder why our dog has started to be difficult with strangers or people trying to touch them!

We do need to have some perspective around how our puppies and dogs are groomed. It is not a natural thing that dogs do to each other, or are born understanding, so to expect our puppies to just accept and get on with it is not fair. I firmly believe that when you take your puppy to the groomer, and even your adult dog, you should make it very clear that you do not want the standard 'breed groom', you want what is right for your puppy or dog. Many groomers will get caught up in doing the expected breed groom. This comes from a book that is taught when you are a groomer – that each breed will have a certain look that should be maintained. This standard look doesn't matter at all. What does matter is that your dog is comfortable, can see clearly (no fur over its eyes) and is happy.

An example is a Cocker Spaniel that 'should' have feathering on their legs for showing, but if you have a family pet that is in and out of lakes, long grass and bushes, you would be far better to clip that feathering as it makes it so much easier to find burrs, grass seeds and to brush out any foreign bodies that could cause health problems. Function over looks is always so much more important in my opinion. The perfect example being the Bedlington Terrier and the huge tuft left on its face in grooming that isn't practical for a dog who needs to use its eyes. So do make this clear to your groomer when you take your puppy in and bring images of what you would like your dog to look like rather than relying on their instinct, as it will be breed based, not practicality based.

If your dog is going to need to go to the groomers every eight weeks and lives for fifteen years, your dog will need to go to the groomer approximately ninety times in their lifetime. And each grooming appointment may last an average of two hours – so that is 180 hours of time your puppy is going to spend at the hands of someone who can have a large impact on your dog's handling abilities, their relationship to being touched and feelings towards humans approaching them. So do not write it off as simply 'going to the groomers'.

CHAPTER FIVE

Your Puppy on the Go

SOCIALISATION

Working with hundreds of dogs over the years, I've realised that owners are really confused about socialisation. We seem to have bought into the idea that socialising a puppy means exposing them to absolutely everything when we bring them home. Whereas socialisation is a process that begins from the day your puppy is born, from their interactions with their mother, their litter, their breeder and the home they grow up in. A puppy, like a human baby, is absorbing information about the world around them every day. So when you get your puppy, it is your job to continue this process of learning and absorbing in a kind and respectful way. And that is what I'm here to help you with. The main thing for you to take away from this section is that socialising your puppy is not a contest or a checklist. It is not about doing, seeing and touching as much as possible in a few short weeks.

The primary socialisation period is when your puppy is still with its mother, up to around eight weeks of age. This period is incredibly important and why the breeder you choose has such a big impact too. If your breeder is doing a beautiful job of raising them in their home, around household noises like the TV, the washing machine, the radio and Nutribullet, then you have a great starting point to spring from. However, socialisation is more complicated than just exposure to household noises. We need to be paying attention to the ways your puppy has experienced life until the day you pick them up. Let me give you some examples:

- The puppy-farmed dog who was raised with its litter and mother. This puppy interacts with its litter and mother but there will be little to no human contact and what contact there is may be abusive or fear-inducing. The humans may deliver some food but the mother may be scared and wary, which means the puppies will follow this model of behaviour. They will bond very heavily with each other and see dogs as good, but humans as not so good or necessary. Which is why it shouldn't be strange when these puppies turn into adult dogs that are fear-aggressive or reactive and struggle so hugely with humans, human eye contact or human interactions.

- The puppy that was raised in the home with four children under the age of eight years old. In theory we can look at children being in the home as positive. However, it is only a plus point if those kids have been taught to be respectful, not to manhandle and breach boundaries with the puppies. Otherwise, it can work in the exact opposite way, with puppies who view children as a negative because the children of the home were allowed free access to the puppy pen, to scoop them up and carry them around with total disregard to what the puppy actually wanted.

• A solo puppy. A puppy that was the only survivor in its litter can have benefits and challenges, depending on how the puppy is raised. If the breeder has other dogs that the puppy can learn from and be around, then these solo dogs can be brilliant additions as they tend to be pretty independent. But if a breeder has a solo puppy and only the mother, it can make that puppy's learning pretty limited, as it will then greatly depend on what the mum's personality is like and what she tolerates. I have a client with a solo Labrador who is such a great dog, because his mum was brilliant and his breeder had several other dogs of varying ages so he was raised by them all. This meant he was, at a young age, very used to interacting with different dogs and understanding his manners.

Whichever way you slice it, socialisation goes back to remembering that your breeder or re-homer is key. They play a huge role in the socialisation of your puppy before you even pick it up and become involved. So please really consider this. To help you, here are some questions you can ask your breeder to find out how much they know about socialisation and how active they are being with their side of the work:

- *Where are the puppies sleeping, playing and toileting?* You want to hear that they have exposure to different surfaces, e.g. tiles, carpet and grass. This is teaching them, from a few weeks of age, about surface differentiation and that surface changes aren't to be feared. This is key if you are raising a dog in a city or urban environment where the surfaces underfoot change all the time.

- *Have the puppies been exposed to the outdoor world, e.g. going into a pen on the grass, onto the patio, for drives in the car?* This is important because although we have to be careful around putting them on the ground when tiny, puppies do need to learn and experience the outside world. It can be deeply traumatic for a new puppy to be taken away when it has never been outside the bubble of being with its mother, littermates and a single room or pen.

- *Has the breeder done any grooming with the puppies?* That can be as simple as trimming their toe fur or giving them baths in the sink or brushing them. If you have a dog that is going to need to be groomed a great deal (e.g. a Toy Poodle), I would expect your breeder to have begun some work on this and to be able to show you what they have done. You want to make sure their handling isn't severe, as this can cause issues later. Do ask for videos of your puppy being groomed so you can check on it.

- *Have the puppies been exposed to the entire home?* As the puppies get older and before you collect them, e.g. at five to eight weeks, I'd be expecting them to start being given a bit of freedom in safe rooms, such as the kitchen when the breeder is cooking or doing some laundry. We want to check that our puppies haven't simply been crated and penned in for eight weeks as that just isn't normal or real life. So ask how that has worked and what they do when given this freedom. Again, ask for videos and photos and look at where your puppy is and what they are getting up to. Is your puppy interested in exploring or do they sit frozen to the floor with anxiety?

- *Has the puppy encountered different objects, toys, etc.?* You want to see that your breeder has gently exposed your puppy and its litter to new objects, toys and other items as that can greatly increase their ability to be resilient and handle stress. These objects can be raw bones, hanging objects, cardboard boxes to pull at, different bowls of different textures – it really shouldn't be complicated, but these tiny details are actually crucial and it's really important for you to look out for and ask about them. In the Puppy Culture guidelines, you can read just how this should be carried out by a breeder to ensure puppies are curious, interested and resilient when it comes to exploring new objects that they haven't encountered before.

Now, let's assume you feel really happy with your breeder and they have done a brilliant job of raising fun-loving, cheerful, resilient, confident little puppies who should be a joy to bring home. Now the responsibility turns to you. And that can feel incredibly daunting and anxiety-inducing. I often have clients who feel like a deer in the headlights at this point, as the level of responsibility truly sinks in – this feeling can still be the same even if you've taken on an older rescue puppy. I want to equip you with the information you need to move forward in this period (eight to twelve/thirteen weeks-ish). The main things you need to remember are:

- Little and often! When it comes to new experiences for your puppy, you are going to be aiming for little and often rather than long and all the time.
- Neutral rather than exciting. You are aiming for neutral encounters and reactions. We don't need every inter-action to be sunshine and rainbows, but we do want to avoid your puppy experiencing fear, being scared, panicked and overwhelmed.
- Be selective. Socialisation is not about introducing your puppy to everyone and everything. You should be selective, based on your lifestyle, family, set-up and environment you live in. For example, someone living in a tiny hamlet in the countryside doesn't really need to worry about public transport usage as they are likely to simply use their car due to their location being quite rural. While someone who lives in the city may need to use public transport daily to take the dog to work with them, so they would begin with short bus or train journeys, or even just a visit to a busy road.
- Take your time. It is crucial to allow your puppy time to ingest, to observe, to watch and learn without having to always interact with things. Watching is really important for them to learn that things they see do not always involve them.

- Avoid sustained time in stimulating environments. You should actively avoid taking your puppy on long days out. I see this all the time in east London, where people believe taking their dog to the market, to the pub, to the park and to the flower store across a four-hour period will be beneficial. It won't be. Your puppy needs time to rest, to process and to 'touch base' by being back in their home with time to sleep in between outings.

- Be wary about bags to carry your puppy in. I don't actually mind them, but do make sure that they are not ones where the dog's head sticks out and everyone and their mother can intrude and pet the puppy without your permission. That is a surefire way to build up a dislike of human contact, by placing a puppy in a situation where they cannot escape and everyone keeps fiddling with them whether they want it or not.

- Don't be scared of putting your puppy on the ground in your garden or other safe places to walk (I don't recommend doing this in parks full of dogs, for example). As stated earlier, I agree with particular vets' recommendations that if we do not socialise our puppies and get them out and about, we risk increasing their chances of behavioural problems that can impact their entire life and yours.

- Vaccinations. These are important to mention here because they will heavily impact how you approach socialisation and what kind of route you take to doing it. I am not a vet, I am a behaviourist. We of course need to keep our puppies safe and I do believe in giving our puppies their primary vaccinations, but after that I believe it gets hazy. I certainly do not believe in yearly boosters and kennel cough up-the-nose treatments, without first checking whether they are needed yet or not. Instead, we should be looking at utilising the technology we have at our fingertips like Titre testing. This is where you can use blood tests to 'check the immune response against the three main diseases they are vaccinated against'* to see if they are still covered from their last booster. This is a far better solution than just constantly giving medication that the dog might not need, and lots of insurance companies will cover this testing.

Scenery Changes

These are one of my favourite things ever when it comes to socialising your puppy. A scenery change isn't taking your dog out for a big adventure, but instead simply changing their environment and allowing them the space to learn and observe.

Before I tell you how to do it, let me tell you why you are going to do it. You are going to facilitate your dog learning about the world without the interruption of dogs, people, kids or cars being able to scare them or make them feel anxious, because the scenery change will all be done from the safety of your front door, or the boot of your car.

---

*www.mulberryhousevets.co.uk/titre-testing/

Every other day, I would advise that you take your puppy either into the car or onto your front doorstep and just sit there. If you are using the car, then you can drive somewhere such as a retail park or a supermarket car park. Park at the back, away from everyone, but somewhere your puppy can watch what's going on. If you are looking at the scenery from your front door then you will simply sit on your doorstep. Make sure your front gate is shut, as we don't want strangers waltzing in. This is about observation.

Then you are going to make sure you have the puppy on their lead and that you have treats. And you are going to sit and just allow your puppy to watch. If they clearly show you that they don't want to be there, for example they are desperate to go back inside or curl up and go to sleep, then perhaps you have chosen the wrong time in their sleeping/energy schedule.

But assuming they're happy with you, you will then sit with your puppy, give them the whole of their lead and just let them sit and watch the world, street, people, cars, cats go by. Don't prompt them, call them, cajole them or otherwise interact with them – let them set the pace. You will do nothing except . . . when they remember you are alive, and they turn round and glance at you or look in your direction, you toss a treat to them where they are stood or give it directly. With this action you are rewarding their 'switch off' from the distraction and their 'reconnection' with you, but without actively asking for it.

If owners did this from very early on, we would have far more dogs that are understanding of the world, connected to their owner and interested in a positive way about what the world offers. Because these scenery changes offer so much for a tiny puppy. They allow a different surface to stand on, new things to learn about and time and leisure to gauge whether these new things are good, bad or neutral. The puppy learns to connect with you when outside of the home, and they get all the sniffs just from standing there, experiencing the world in a way we will never understand.

Scenery changes are something you should be incorporating and using every other day. I even use these with senior dogs who can't get out and about as much as they used to, but who still need exploration and stimulation.

Your puppy will feel tired after doing a session like this (a scenery change may last ten minutes or thirty-five minutes, depending on the age and abilities of your puppy), because it involves a great deal of mental stimulation. If you have a puppy-proofed front garden and a gate, you could start to use a long line or let your puppy off entirely. I'd start doing this more around the twelve to fourteen weeks mark, to allow more freedom, but still rewarding their eye contact, switching off and reconnection with you. Your puppy may show you they have had enough by wanting to get back inside, which is why I often advise my clients to sit on the doorstep where they're able to, with the door open so your puppy can choose. Or they may come and want to go to sleep on you, or you may notice their behaviour switches from a snuffling, observational, interested puppy into a frantic and feral puppy, and that would show you it's time to go in and get some rest.

WALKING YOUR PUPPY

I think that the walking aspect of owning a puppy is something that many owners dreamed of. Then they can feel disappointed when they step out for the first time with their puppy and realise it isn't just a flowing walk to get a coffee. Instead it is a stop–start, sniffing, lunging, sitting down, pulling walk that takes thirty minutes to do what would usually take ten!

Don't worry if you fall into that camp. The majority of my clients do. An easy way to overcome this is to calculate what your usual walk time would be and then to allow two or three times the amount of time. Then you won't be late, and you won't be feeling hacked off either! And this won't last for ever, but it's a crucial period where your puppy needs to take time to absorb their new surroundings.

The thing you have to realise is that you can't rush a puppy. Not if you want them to be a well-developed, confident dog in the future. I know that might sound frustrating, but you are going to have to make adaptations when you get a puppy, and this is one of them.

When you have a young puppy, you are going to be looking at three twenty-minute outdoor sessions per day. By that I mean leaving the house and exploring. Not every twenty-minute outdoor session will be a walk, but it should be time spent out of the house learning about the world.

When you have an older puppy, you can start to increase your walking times and out-of-the-house times. This will depend on your dog's nature, energy levels, breed and breed traits.

We do not want to be over-exerting our dogs, but we also don't want to be under-stimulating them either. There are no hard and fast rules, despite what some might say – like the five minutes' walk per month of age rule, which I do not believe in. Instead, we need to be very aware of our pup's bone development and growth plates, and we need to tailor our outdoor excursions to that. So, for example, you may decide to carry them to the park and then spend your 'walk' time out in the park. Or you may decide to spend one of your outdoor excursions just in a friend's garden so that the puppy can explore but not walk very far.

In my experience, the real danger to your dog's growth plates is not so much from walks. We actually need to be more careful about the way our kids handle our dogs (not encouraging them to jump up and run around like loons). We need to not allow other dogs to knock over our puppy, or wrestle with them in a high-impact way. We need to think about the surfaces we have at home that they can slip, splat and fall over on. We should not be lobbing balls in the house or outside for puppies to chase after and stop abruptly, as this sends all the physical impact of that emergency stop up the paws, into the leg joints and up to the shoulders. All of those things can be more damaging to your puppy's growing body than simply walking it on its lead in a straight line!

I would vary your walks and where you go. You want to teach your puppy that walks are exploration time, a time to be active and use their nose, do training and connect with you. So how you walk your puppy from the first day will impact that. If you simply take your puppy to the park and let them run around with other dogs, you are setting up their expectation that a walk means running away from you and chasing after other dogs. And that creates a heat-seeking missile that simply focuses on dogs instead of you.

How we begin taking our dog out and about impacts our pups and their future behaviour and expectations, so do think carefully about what kind of walks you will be doing over the coming years. For example, it may be important that your dog can happily trot through the city and do sniffy walks on concrete, as well as enjoying big romps in the long grass, so we need to mix it up from day one so that it is what they expect.

Do select your parks and where you walk carefully. If you only take them to dog parks or places where there are a lot of dogs, then you are going to drastically increase your dog's distraction levels and make it harder for them to focus on you. Thinking about the time of day that you visit is also important. Avoid the busiest times when your puppy is small, as you do not want your puppy to feel bombarded by people, dogs, scooters, cyclists and children every time they set foot outside of the house. We need to introduce these things carefully. And if your puppy is a bit older (e.g. six months plus) you need to be very aware that your puppy is going to start testing their boundaries and going further afield. So where their abilities may have been great in the park, they are going to deteriorate and you need to be prepared to go back to the early days and build those foundations again.

At ten months old, you should expect to see that your dog's exercise and stimulation requirements increase. Many owners feel bewildered when their pup reaches this age, but it is important to understand that your puppy is now capable of more and needs more. That does not mean you need to be running them into the ground. But it does mean you need to think about how your day looks for your dog, when you are exercising them and what stimulation you are providing for them. I recently saw a client with a Cockapoo who at thirteen months old was struggling with settling down in the evenings. After some discussion, I realised that his main walk was first thing in the morning and then he would get a couple of around-the-block pee breaks later on, but that was it. So we added in another hour in the late afternoon and it made a world of difference. His unsettled behaviour was as simple as him needing an outlet for his afternoon energy. When not provided with one, he became a problem.

What we have to remember is that walks are our dog's time. They don't get to choose when they leave the house or where they go, so we need to make sure that walks satisfy, reward and fulfil our dog's needs. Which is why street walks on the lead can be so boring for many breeds, as they want to explore, roam, sniff, scent, get into the world of grass, mud and more. Street walks can be OK when we have young pups who we are teaching about the world, but after about sixteen weeks of age, they can become a bit boring. Not for all dogs, but do regularly assess what makes your dog tick. So if you get back from a street walk and they are wired and need to gallivant around the house, then you can assume the walk either didn't hit the spot or it was too overwhelming so they don't know what to do with themselves.

On the flip side, if your puppy comes home from an excursion or walk and sleeps for hours, then you know it was way too much. The point is not to exhaust them so that they cannot do anything else. Which is just one of the reasons I don't recommend dog walkers and day care for dogs under the age of two years unless it is a very small setting with selected dogs or solo care: the dogs become overstimulated and overtired to the point of exhaustion.

Walking your dog can feel hard, and if I'm being honest, it is. You are taking out an animal that wants to do totally different things from what you want to do! So your walks need to be about understanding how you can make them work for both of you. You need to revisit your dog's breed traits and make sure you are really thinking about what their particular breed needs.

For example, a Dachshund needs to be able to frolic, sniff, snuffle and trot along. A Working Cocker Spaniel needs to be able to have large areas to roam, to get into undergrowth, to go through long grass, to look for things and find them. We often dismiss these things, but they are absolutely key to raising a happy, contented dog.

Loose-lead walking

Lastly, loose-lead walking, which is training your dog in the park with a 3- to 4-metre lead attached to its collar or harness. There's no getting away from the fact that this kind of training is laborious and time-consuming. While holding the lead in a place where there aren't too many other distractions, you will reward your puppy for being next to you, looking up at you and walking near you. You don't call them, prompt them or cajole them, you simply capture what they will do naturally as an eight-week-old puppy who is looking to you for cues on how to behave. This is another reason to be putting them down on the ground and starting your training, as your puppy is only going to get bolder and less likely to stay close to you. You really want to begin that work from day dot, when your puppy is going to want to stay close to you.

If you are going to use a harness, do not believe that it will stop a dog pulling. It won't. You should choose to use a collar or harness based on your dog and their comfort level. There are many harnesses on the market that can cause huge musculoskeletal issues because of the way they prohibit shoulder movement, or they sit right behind the front legs and cause an impact that way. Your dog's harness should allow full shoulder movement so that the joint can rotate. A harness should not go across their shoulder and top of legs or cover it. I see a great deal of bull breeds put in them because they look heavy duty. They do not need them either, and they will create more harm than they solve if they cover the shoulders and don't allow shoulder movement and rotation. The other harnesses to be aware of are the ones that go over their head and have a lot of material, so they can look pretty and come in lovely colourways but they create the same impact as a collar, as essentially those harnesses act like a giant fabric collar covering the top parts of their chest and body and spread the impact from any pulling.

A collar is actually fine, provided your dog isn't pulling, and again that is something to begin work on. You do need to make sure their collar is comfortable, not too tight and that it doesn't prohibit any movement or feel too heavy. With a well-fitting collar you should be able to get at least a couple of fingers between the collar and their neck and it should not be able to fit over their head.

For walking your dog, you should think about having a long-line (5 metres long) and a street-walking lead (2–3 metres long). The street one is for teaching loose-lead walking in a non-pulling manner. And the long line is for teaching independence and showing a puppy what you want it to do when out and about and when it has more freedom, e.g. in the field or park.

RECALL

Your dog coming to you when you call them is not hard-wired into their brain from birth. This was something I realised that people believed when I used to run puppy classes. Owners of puppies presumed that their puppy should 'just know' what to do when they said 'come'. Yet they hadn't actually done any work or association-forming or building of the foundations to teach their puppy. This is where we will begin.

When it comes to recall, it's super-important to know what motivates your dog. Essentially, when teaching recall you want whatever you're offering to be the most exciting thing your dog can imagine. You do not want to be offering your dog a stale old bit of kibble when another dog is offering them a zoom around the park for ten minutes: you just can't compete. Understanding what you are working with for your dog is absolutely key.

The first thing to work out before we proceed any further is: what motivates my puppy and how can I utilise this kindly and fairly? In order to ascertain this, we need to be studying and observing our puppy's natural inclinations and abilities. Let me give you some client examples.

Ruby the Weimaraner loves to carry things, catch balls and get her nose stuck into undergrowth, and adores having freedom to run.

Happy the Tibetan Terrier loves rubber toys to pull apart, is only bothered by treats if he is hungry (otherwise will ignore them, no matter how lush they are), and loves to jump high and use his mouth when he is excited. He loves to paddle in shallow water.

So if we take these two dogs, you can see that they have very different likes in their life and things that interest them that we can use for training, to teach them things and to make sure their life is happy.

Where Ruby loves to catch a ball, it is the ideal reward for her for sticking close and not running off or as a recall reward, but if I gave this reward to Happy, he wouldn't even bother picking it up, let alone playing with it. Therefore it wouldn't reward his sticking close or recall, it would actually demotivate him. If when he recalled to me, I played a jumping game, he would be extremely happy and this would bring him joy and motivate him to come back when I call.

What motivates our puppies differs and it is worth spending some time writing ideas down, looking at how motivating it is on a scale of one to ten, and if it is only motivating in certain environments. Some dogs will love to play tugger games in the house where they feel safe and secure, but if you try to do it outside they will not engage. It is all about understanding what makes your dog tick and not someone else's in the park. Which is why strangers' well-meaning advice doesn't work most of the time or isn't applicable to your puppy.

Lastly, it is important to have a variety of options, otherwise we just rely heavily on one option and we can end up creating dogs that won't do anything else other than just fetch a ball. Dogs are sensory creatures, they adore sniffing, snuffling, watching, jumping, mouthing, touching, listening and learning – so you do have a gazillion options open to you. And this is an area I adore helping my clients with, to empower them to unlock the potential with their puppy.

It is important to point out that your dog's name is not their recall cue. Their name is what you use to get their attention. In the same way, if you said my name across a room, I wouldn't come running immediately, I'd simply look over to see what you wanted and await direction/conversation/input. The same is true with our puppies. We want to teach them their name so they know when we are referring to them and singling them out. Then we can give them further input about what to do next.

Teaching a recall cue is rather similar, in that primarily we just want to teach an automatic response. The puppy needs to learn that when a cue is given they respond and they get rewarded brilliantly for that response. If we start this cue–response–reward from day one, we can have this built in very quickly. We can of course teach it when they are older puppies too but if you have an eight-week-old puppy, then make the most of having this head start.

First of all, think about the cue you would like to use, e.g. 'come'/'here'/'back'/'apple' – the word doesn't matter too much so long as you have a consistent one.

When your puppy is tiny (I'd start this at eight weeks if you can) and they are stood looking up at you, simply place a little treat on the floor where you are standing. As they scoff it, take a few steps away, when they follow you and come towards you, place a treat down on the floor and repeat. After doing this five times, you are going to start using your recall cue when your puppy has finished the treat and is beginning to walk towards you out of their own choice. So, for example:

- Treat on floor.
- Walk away.
- Puppy follows.
- You say 'come' and put a treat on the floor.
- Repeat twenty times every day.

If your dog is highly motivated by this game, then you could do all twenty treats in one session. If your dog is slower or still sussing it out, you could do four sessions across a day of five treats each.

Start off at home. Then you are going to start practising in your hallway, then in the back garden, then in the front garden, then on the little green near your home, then in the shop car park, then in the park. Your puppy will be learning that the command is the same in lots of different environments.

You will find that your puppy picks this up super-quickly. And then, as discussed, they will get older and start testing boundaries. This is when they just want to run off towards every single dog, child, scooter or person they see. But it is an important foundation that you need to start with, build on and know that one day it will be useful again when their brain matures and they remember all the things you taught them when they were tiny! In the meantime, you are also going to need to be doing some hard graft with recall that can at best feel wonderful and at worst feel like your puppy doesn't care and isn't the slightest bit interested in you. So for those occasions I've made some suggestions on how you can start to handle recall depending on what development phase your beloved puppy is in.

Recall month by month

In this section you are going to start to understand why the age of puppies can impact recall and how they respond to you. It should help you feel less helpless and more patient and proactive!

NOUGHT TO SIX MONTHS

In this phase, you should practise having your puppy off their lead, as they will want to be close and stay near you as the world is still very much a new and intimidating place for them. So, as long as it is safe to do so, you could do five minutes on lead, five minutes off lead and keep alternating. Reward them for following you, reward them for giving you eye contact, reward them for sniffing something and when they choose to run back to you, give them treats.

Basically, we want to be setting up the idea that staying close is cool, and that they can sniff stuff and explore but should keep coming back to make contact with us – and let them know that this is a great choice by encouraging them with treats and toys. Don't use their recall cue when they don't need it, as you will wear it out.

Don't practise recall with your puppy where you stand a distance apart and keep calling your dog between you. It is boring for your dog and it doesn't replicate actual recall scenarios. Instead, work on letting your dog know that hanging out with you is where the good stuff is.

SIX TO TWELVE MONTHS

Expect it all to start to go south as your puppy gets more curious, bolder and ready to explore and bowl off without you. This period can feel really tiring and triggering for some people as it isn't what they thought puppy ownership would be like. It can feel like several exhausting months of running around the park saying 'sorry' to everyone!

You need to hold your nerve and know that this is a developmental phase, but you do still need to be actively working on the puppy's recall, keeping them close and not allowing them to run off. So this may be the phase when you start using the 5-metre long line more regularly. This will be when you begin to assess where you walk your puppy – where is too dog dense, where is too distracting, where is full of owners who pay no attention to their dogs? All these things become important when you are weighing up where and when you walk your puppy off lead or on a long line. If you are taking your puppy to a full-on, dog-packed park full of people then you can only expect one thing – overstimulation, an inability to listen, and frustration and upset from your side.

You will honestly have days when you come home crying from a walk or sit in the car and have some tears. Just know that we have all been there. Some years ago I fostered a six-month-old Boxer x Great Dane called Henry. He once escaped from my car boot and ran across six football pitches to reach a Rottweiler on the other side. I literally sobbed just watching him, as there was no way I could run that far in time to retrieve him and stop the interaction. I had no idea what was going to happen and I was so angry at myself for not realising that he could squeeze through the gap in the window while I was getting my other dog out of the car. But this taught me something that I'm now imparting to you. If your dog does not have any recall or is struggling with listening, then either don't put them in situations where you know they can't do what you want them to do. Or, if you have to take them into a situation or environment that you know they aren't equipped to deal with, lower your expectations: put them on a long line and reward the tiniest of details. If in a quiet field they will stop, turn around and look at you, then absolutely reward them, but if in a dog park they merely throw you a quick glance over their shoulder, still reward this big time. As I tell my clients, when it is harder for a puppy, make it easier. It will make your life and their life so much more enjoyable as you are being realistic and still capturing tiny things that will lead to big things.

Rather like not expecting a teenage son to come downstairs at 6 a.m. for school with a smile on their face, happy to see you and full of the joys of life, expectation is everything!

A really good system to establish is to alternate your days so that you have a day where you go somewhere with the sole purpose of training and showing your dog what you would like them to do, and the next day go somewhere super-empty where you can let your dog have freedom and just reward the check-ins. Do not try to do everything every day or else you will fail and be upset and wonder what you are doing with your life. Believe me, I've been there.

TWELVE TO EIGHTEEN MONTHS

You will start to notice moments when your puppy didn't run off on the walk at the slightest distraction. You'll recognise that you had two days of happy outings instead of dreading the walks. This progress may then be followed with a tricky day, but you will see signs, rather like when you see the signs of spring – a daffodil here, a tulip there. The signs will start to show that you are coming out of the trickier phase and going into a section where the things you taught at nought to six months are coming back to your puppy. The work you did on the long line and with quieter walks starts to impact how your dog views a walk.

You may still be struggling with your puppy's excitement and distraction, but it will feel more manageable and you will know that you need to provide things like a run around in the long grass before letting them off lead or else they will badger each dog they see. Or you'll know that you need to be alternating where you walk to provide different stimulation because your dog is a busy dog who needs variety. Perhaps you need to make sure you get your dog to 'sniffy' walks because it really helps them calm down. (This applies to most dogs, by the way.)

By this stage, you will start to feel a bit more confident in predicting your dog. They certainly won't feel 'reliable', but you will feel like you know them more and understand them better. If you have a big-breed dog, they may still be behind developmentally, so just push this phase on by a few months and it will feel more relevant for you as big breeds can be more like two years old by the time they get there.

Now we need to think about how we actually go about working on your puppy's recall abilities. Here are some do's and don'ts when it comes to teaching your puppy to come back to you when you call them.

Do not:

- Keep calling your dog if they aren't listening or aren't able to listen, as you will just wear out your recall cue. The same goes with whistles. I watched a woman in the park the other day with her little Border Terrier puppy. She blew her whistle around six times as her dog ran off to play with other dogs. Not once did the dog notice it, respond or return. She needed to stop using that cue, as the lack of response proves it means nothing to your dog and you need to go back to the drawing board.
- Walk your dog in the same place or park every day. Your dog will get bored and it will really impact your recall.
- Simply stop letting them off lead if they aren't listening. Instead, adjust where you are walking and how distracting it is. For example, renting a

field for an hour with friends is often very reason-
able, where it is fully fenced and designed to allow
dogs to have freedom, a roam and snuffle when they
aren't yet reliable in other unfenced parks. These
tend to range from £7 to £18 an hour, depending
on the location, the size and the resources. This
space will allow you and your puppy time to relax
and you can still capture and reward the behaviours
you want from your dog.

- Believe that just because your dog can do it at home,
  they will be able to do it outside. We have to teach
  our puppies about recall in many, many locations and
  spend a great deal of time 'generalising' a behaviour
  so that they realise it applies to all locations.

- Stop your dog being a dog. We want to give a puppy
  freedom to explore, we want them to be curious, to
  sniff, to snuffle, to root around. The idea is not to
  have a robot, but to have a dog who can be a dog
  and to be able to call it back should you need to.

- Allow your dog to run up to and into other dogs. If
  another dog is on a lead, it means very clearly that
  your dog is not welcome to be in their face. That dog
  may be aggressive, it may be anxious, it may be unwell,
  it may be recovering from an operation. It is your
  responsibility to keep your puppy with you as soon
  as you see the other owner has their dog on their
  lead. If my dog is off lead and I see another dog on
  lead, I will immediately call my dog to me and either
  hold them and let them pass or put mine on the lead
  and keep out of their way. And I expect others to
  do the same when I have my dog on the lead.

- Put your dog on the lead for any recall failure. If your dog has run off, don't simply grab it and shove it back on the lead the moment it returns. I know it can be hard to keep a level head at this stage, but these 'moments' are still great learning experiences of what we want our puppies to do. So go up to where your puppy has run off to, stick your hand with a stinking treat in it into your puppy's face and if they so much as look up, give them the treat. Keep repeating this as you are showing your puppy that even when it's super-hard and super-distracting, paying attention to you (even if it's a glimpse) is where they want to be. By all means clip the lead on so they cannot just run off again, but you can't end the treats there, you need to keep supplying them so that your puppy learns it is great sticking with you and isn't clambering at the end of the lead to get as far away from you as possible. You won't see an immediate change, but these learning experiences do shift how and when your puppy listens and responds over time.
- Don't forget to take toys out with you. In order to reward your puppy when out and about, toys need to be a part of your repertoire even into adulthood. When we remove play and toys from our park trips, it can signal the death knell for a dog wanting to stay close to you.

Do:

- Dish out treats and more treats and more treats after that. Focus on building brilliant foundations

– rewarding your puppy for being near you, looking at you, stopping to check in with you, running back to you, seeing where you are. You will do this for life if you want a dog who is going to stay close. Do not be tempted once they are 'good' at it to stop doing it, or you will see a decline. Just like if you were doing a job really well and then your boss decided to decrease your pay because you now know how to do the job and can do it really well. That wouldn't be fair, would it?

• Set your puppy up to succeed by choosing suitable places to walk that make the walk enjoyable for you too. Often we get caught up in what we 'think' a walk should look like, but there are no set rules. Don't worry about what others are doing with their puppy or dog, your puppy is your puppy and their journey may just look different.

• Be honest with yourself. If you are tired or having a day when you are struggling, then don't take your puppy to a hard place to walk. Instead go somewhere where all dogs must be on a lead, or to a field where you can sit and put them on a long line while you throw treats into the long grass. Make life easy on days when it feels hard.

• Be prepared that some days will be long-line days and others will be off-lead days and that is OK.

• Work on motivation regularly. Notice your dog's likes and reflect that in their recall training.

• Realise that your dog's breed, breeding and genetics hugely impact their abilities. If you need a reminder, go back and look up what your breed or breeds were bred to do, and think about how that will impact their instincts and what you need to be working on. For example, if you have a dog designed to chase, spend your early days working on teaching a 'wait' cue before you release them to run. Don't use chase games from day one and don't presume that being allowed to just chase other dogs as a tiny puppy won't cause issues later on. We have to keep bringing it back to what our dog was bred to do: stop fighting it, and instead work with it and be realistic.

MEETING OTHER DOGS

When you're walking down the street, do you stop and interact with every person you pass? Do you insist they speak to you even if they don't want to? Do you get in their way and force them to notice you? I'm assuming not! Yet somehow people seem to think this behaviour is totally fine when it comes to how dogs interact with each other.

We have to look into the future and think about how we want our dog to be around other dogs. Most of my clients say that they want their dog to be friendly, to have a friend or two that they enjoy playing with, and to be able to walk past other dogs without lunging and barking. If these are our aims, how do we go about achieving them?

A great start is to consider which dogs your friends and family own or live with that would be good, appropriate role models for your puppy to meet and walk with. We are looking for dogs that are not going to bully, overwhelm or react to your puppy. Dogs who can say hi, maybe have a little play but then potter around and sniff and do their own thing. Puppies need to learn that interacting with another dog doesn't mean constant play or wrestling or badgering another dog. Learning to spend time with another dog without doing much is an underrated skill for your puppy to develop.

Role-model dogs have a great relationship with their owners and can listen and show your puppy how to do the same. Our puppies are social learners, so don't kid yourself that the dogs your dog hangs out with won't matter, because they do.

It is wise to consider the effect of a dog walker or day care on your puppy. As I've mentioned, I prefer they aren't used until your puppy is much older, around two years of age. If they are used, it should ideally be very small scale, so that they are only walked alone or with one or two other well-suited dogs. Otherwise we run very high risks of issues developing that may be irreversible. I have noticed that resource guarding – getting possessive around food or toys – is something I see commonly start in day care settings, where there is a lot of competition between dogs.

We must also look at how our dog's days are structured in day care settings. For young dogs (under two years), free access to play with other dogs all the time can become an issue. A puppy that is free to bother other dogs may get repeatedly told off by them. This isn't something we want all the time, as at some point your dog won't tolerate the telling off and will snap back. Then we have a fight on our hands that was entirely avoidable.

Many day care settings will insist on neutering and spaying to be able to walk or have the dog, which I understand, but considering I wouldn't generally advise doing this until a puppy is much older, I certainly wouldn't want you to do it earlier just to be able to keep them in a care setting as that can impact their entire life and their behaviour for ever.

When you see another dog in the street or the park and your puppy is on the lead, get in the habit of showing them what you want them to do. Don't wait for your puppy to do something else to then be annoyed by it. They are a puppy, they are going to try things out, so get ahead of the behaviour. Use treats to teach them to walk past another dog without interacting, rewarding every step and rewarding them again as the other dog walks off. Show them how to walk past dogs from the moment you start taking them out and it will soon become second nature, if we start teaching it early.

Plan walks and outings and meet-ups with dogs you really like and enjoy spending time with. To teach your puppy how to walk near them, you will probably need to parallel walk a few times before you can have any hope of actually walking together. Take the dogs on walks where there are interesting things to do, e.g. sniffing in the long grass rather than just taking them to flat playing fields with nothing else to do, as otherwise your puppy is much more likely to be annoying to another dog because they are the most interesting thing there.

Choose a couple of dogs that your dog likes to play with and start to work really hard on teaching your puppy to listen to their name when you say it while they are playing. Reward them for looking at you while that other dog is around, and then let them go back in and play.

Stop the play if it gets too full on and finish the walk with calm walking, ignoring each other. You cannot expect your puppy to be allowed to play like a Tasmanian devil with certain dogs and then understand that she can't do it with every dog. We do need to be selective over who our puppy is going out on walks and socialising with.

If you are struggling to keep your puppy with you out on walks while off lead, then it may be time to bring back the 5-metre long line and use it properly, i.e. not just letting it trail around after them! If your puppy is struggling with recall, then you have to be proactive in how you use the long line, which is to hold the end and let them have the freedom to sniff and run and snuffle, but as soon as you see their body posture change, as soon as you see them go into an alert pose and fixate on a dog in the distance, then stand still, hold on and wait for your puppy to remember that you are alive and on the other end of that long line. As soon as your puppy turns to check in with you, looks at you, sniffs the ground or spins around, you are going to explode with joy and treats and toys! You are going to be like one of those celebratory emojis on a phone, dishing out rewards to mark that incredible decision your puppy made: to look to you rather than just run off.

I can't over-emphasise how important this kind of training is for our puppies of all ages. To allow them time to figure it out, to let them give it a go and then we simply capture the very clever thing they have chosen.

Lastly, it is important to mention here that it is not another dog's job to tell your puppy off, to reprimand them, to 'put them in their place' as I hear many owners say. It is your puppy, it is your training, it is your job to make sure your puppy is not a menace to other dogs, while also finding suitable dogs to learn from. We need to teach that there are many dogs they will never meet or interact with. It is not your puppy's given right to leap at, lunge at or jump on any dog in their sightline. By allowing your puppy to badger, chase or aggravate another dog when you can see they aren't happy or don't want it (e.g. trying to walk away, turning their head, moving to avoid the puppy), you are going to create problems with your puppy's dog fixations that will only get worse. You will also create reactivity and aggression issues for the dog who has to keep telling off or shouting at puppies who aren't respecting their boundaries. That is not fair on anyone.

HOW DO I KNOW IF MY PUPPY IS SCARED?

One thing I have realised through working with thousands of clients and their puppies is how hard many owners can find it to figure out what fear looks like in our dogs. With that in mind, here are some ways that your puppy may show you fear, but please note that this is not an exhaustive list:

- Rolling over when dogs or people approach. We have to be really careful with this one. Owners tend to think that this is their dog showing they want their tummy rubbed. In situations like this, it doesn't tend to be: it is most often a dog feeling intimidated, and you will need to get them out of the situation.

- Trying to get away. This can sometimes look like they are being chased by other dogs, but it can actually be them trying to escape while the dog won't leave them alone. You will need to intervene.
- Turning their head away and not wanting to interact with the person/dog/child/stimulus.
- Are their eyes darting around, popping out, not daring to make eye contact? That shows your dog is scared.
- Being skittish, darting or not knowing what to do with themselves. This shows that your puppy is struggling and can't figure out what to do. Create distance for them and let them have space.
- Puppies that are hiding, won't come out of a space and don't want to walk past something are all indicating that they are not comfortable. Do not force them. And do not pull them out or you may end up being bitten.

It is worth mentioning here a dog's ladder of aggression or, as I call it, the traffic-light system. This is how a well-socialised and well-bred dog will show their emotions and whether they like something or not. (Dogs do not use the same system as people, but I will draw some parallels between us to help you understand what I'm trying to illustrate.)

We often say things like 'it came out of nowhere' in response to a dog biting, growling and nipping, when the exact opposite is true. A heap of signs and signals were probably given out but because they aren't how we communicate, we as humans skip over them. This isn't usually through ignorance but because we are so tuned in to only thinking about how humans do things that we do not see what the dog is trying to do. Let me help you understand and unpick this a bit more . . .

Here is the traffic-light system to understand your puppy's behaviour:

Traffic Light	Dog – a child is present and won't leave them alone, keeps following and trying to sit next to and pet them	Human – on a bus and a stranger stands too close and makes you feel uncomfortable
GREEN LIGHT	• Gets up and walks off • Slow turn of head away • Lip licking • Stress yawning • Shifts positions • May jump up at child as it feels overwhelmed • Comes to you for help • Ears go back • Eyes are worried	• Step away to create space • Face away from the person • Put your headphones in • Avoid making eye contact • Ask person to give some space

AMBER LIGHT	• Turns head away repeatedly in both directions • Hides under something, e.g. a table • Lip curls to show side teeth • May bark • Will be restless • May jump up at you • May growl	• Ask person to give more space in a louder, more irate manner • Use bag to block them • Let out deep breaths/huff and puff • Arms crossed • Repeat asking to create space in an even more irate way, may shout
RED LIGHT	• May nip • May lunge • May bark • May bite • May do all the above and run away	• May shout at the person • May push them • Voices will get raised • May start a fight

As you can see from this table, our dogs do have ways of showing us that something isn't working for them. It is so important that we are tuned in and responsive so that we are able to advocate for our dog and step in.

This table is not a full example of all body postures, but it highlights how we all react when our buttons are pushed, our boundaries are broken and we feel like we have no options. Understanding this for our puppies is absolutely key in order to raise a well-adjusted, well-socialised and happy puppy who likes people, kids and other animals.

Fear when out and about

There can be many reasons why our dogs may feel fear as puppies, and commonly it is because they are in a developmental stage where things are worrisome, as discussed earlier. Or it might be because your puppy has a genetic predisposition to fear due to their breeding, or perhaps their mother was anxious and this has taught them to be anxious too. The main thing to understand is that there is a difference between a puppy who is a little bit unsure about a situation and just needs to figure it all out, and a puppy who is deeply anxious, either paralysed by a situation or reactive because of it. ('Reactive' is a way of describing a dog that is 'reacting' to a situation in a way that feels like an over-reaction to the stimulus.) If you can, try not to tell your puppy off for their reaction, as it will fall on deaf ears, but you also need to bear in mind that reactivity tends to come from a place of fear. Telling them off won't build their trust in you and it won't make them less fearful.

If your puppy is one of the deeply anxious ones due to their breeding, previous trauma or similar, you will need to book in one-to-one tailored time with a behaviourist. A puppy who finds life this challenging requires much more help than I can suggest here. It is a worthwhile investment – a dog living its entire life in fear is no life at all, and if we can help them then we really must. Please do not turn to free videos online as these will not help you in the long term, and they may just make your situation far worse.

There is also the option of medication for severely anxious dogs. Due to their breeding and the way some puppies have been raised, I am seeing many more dogs whose anxiety is very complex and deep-rooted. We do have to acknowledge that the loving care of an owner is not always enough. When we are dealing with a dog who is struggling, unbalanced and who is finding the world a tough place to be, simply loving them will not solve it. In this situation, you do need to reach out for tailored help. It would be worth asking your vet for a referral to a veterinary behaviourist, as they can also dispense suitable medication to help their behaviour.

However, these are extreme examples. For puppies who have had a good start in life and just need a bit of extra help, there is so much that we can do in terms of teaching our anxious puppy that life isn't something to be so worried about.

With a puppy like this, as I've said earlier, it is important to allow time to watch, to observe and not to just rush through life. Puppies of all ages learn by experiencing and observing. If a bin lorry is reversing down your road and that is making your puppy worried, find a place to stand at a distance, where your puppy seems more curious than frightened. Let them show you they feel comfortable and allow them to sit in your arms and watch the bin lorry and learn that it actually isn't scary.

Please do not be tempted to simply pick up your puppy and shove them in the face of what they are fearing. This won't help them trust you and it won't make the thing they are scared of feel less scary. I see people do it when they are introducing their puppy to an adult dog, lowering the shaking puppy to the dog's face to sniff. You will be creating problems for the future with a dog that doesn't feel safe with you, or in new situations.

If your puppy is showing uncertainty about meeting new people, you will have to advocate for your puppy and say that people can't pet it. This can feel mean – who doesn't want to pet a puppy! But it can create fear in a puppy who feels overwhelmed, and it's important to kindly let people know that your puppy needs space. You can stop people from intruding on their personal space by using your legs to block your puppy as they stand behind you, or placing treats by your feet to keep your puppy by you and not out in front. I also like to teach a puppy the middle cue – which is where they go between your legs and either stand or sit to feel protected. To teach this cue, you simply take these steps:

- Stand with your feet well apart.
- Take a treat that your puppy is interested in and, with your puppy stood behind you, bend forward and extend your hand with the treat through your legs.
- Your puppy should come over to your hand and you can reward them a couple of times.
- After a few repetitions, start to move your hand so your puppy follows the treat through your legs.
- Next, you will do the same thing but, as they come through your legs, stop them once they are stood under you, when their head is just past your legs, and reward them for being stationary while stood under your legs.
- Keep practising that position. You can then choose whether you get them to sit or keep them standing. It will be your choice and depends on what your puppy naturally does.

The idea here is that you provide your puppy with a safe place to go where other people aren't going to interfere with them in. These techniques are a great way to help your puppy feel secure and not allow well-meaning dog lovers to ruin the training and socialisation you are attempting to do.

If your puppy is in a situation where it is jumping up at your legs to be picked up, please do pick them up. I have no issue with this whatsoever, and I don't believe in letting dogs 'sort it out themselves', especially when one dog is often much bigger and more intimidating than another. Many of our longer-legged breeds do this at times when they feel unsure, uncomfortable or scared. By pushing them away, we simply reinforce a message that we are not going to help them when they are afraid. That is the last thing we want as the next step may be that your frightened puppy starts to run out of the park or away from you, as they don't trust you to keep them safe.

Lastly, if your dog feels cornered, pestered or over-whelmed in a situation and they snap or growl at another dog or person, do not tell them off for it. The puppy or dog is giving a warning that this situation is too much. Instead of telling off your puppy, look at what led to that behaviour and how can we make sure it isn't allowed to happen again. This might mean giving your dog freedom off lead so that they can choose to get away from other dogs, and not allowing other dogs to jump on, hump or keep sniffing your dog if they are clearly showing they do not want it. Perhaps it might mean not taking your dog with you someplace like a busy pub where you can't keep an eye on what people and their kids are doing. Either way, it is our job to learn what our puppy is telling us, because their behaviour is always trying to inform us.

Reprimanding your puppy for their fear response definitely won't help. Instead, we have to backtrack and look at where signs were given that a situation was becoming too much, e.g. a head turn, a lip curl, a backing away, a licking of the lips.

CHAPTER SIX

Feeding Your Puppy

Thanks to campaigners and medical experts such as Tim Spector, we humans are finally realising that fresher, less processed foods and ingredients are the best way to feed ourselves and our children for health and longevity. Yet I've found that even the family who eats the healthiest diet, full of fresh ingredients, will often feed their dogs nothing more than ultra-processed biscuits in the form of kibble. People do this with the best intentions and are often advised to do so by their vets who recommend prescription-only foods. Please know that what you feed your puppy either supports them or hinders their growth and development. Just as you wouldn't feed a child on a diet exclusively composed of biscuits, nor should you feed your puppy this way – even if those biscuits promise they are grain-free, organic or 'natural'. There are so many better options for your puppy, and so much more we can do to nourish them and help them live a long and healthy life.

WHAT TO FEED YOUR PUPPY

There is a huge amount of conflicting information out there on how to feed your dog, and it can feel hard to know what to do and what is 'best' for your puppy. These are my thoughts and not everyone will agree with them, but I would urge you to think carefully about the way you set your puppy up for its future health and happiness.

When you first bring your puppy home, it's best to keep them on the food the breeder gave you for at least three to seven days. Keep things consistent for the puppy when so much else has changed now you've brought it home. However, I wouldn't advise investing in a big bag of the food your breeder uses unless you are utterly certain it is decent and what you want to use long term. Very few breeders feed fresh, as kibble is cheaper, plus many of the big brands give breeders huge discounts as they know it pays off because breeders then send puppies off with that food into their new households! Puppies raised on the Puppy Culture method I've mentioned before will usually be raised on a fresh diet – another reason to try to find breeders using this methodology.

During your puppy's early days and even beyond, you may have times when your puppy gets an upset stomach. This is really common and can happen for many reasons – stress, emotions, scavenging, etc. It is worth knowing that in chapter sixteen of my previous book, *The Book Your Dog Wishes You Would Read*, I discuss prescription diets in great detail, specifically gastrointestinal foods sold by vet practices. It is worth reading up on this, I think, because it can be tempting to just take the food when at the vets. In my opinion, this food is not the best option if your puppy gets an upset stomach. The contents of the processed gastro food are just that: highly processed. Instead, try feeding them their usual food with a warm bone broth over the top, or cooking a turkey and pumpkin combination to ease the stomach and provide decent gentle ingredients that nourish the gut and intestines. This will make a transition back to their usual food very easy too.

There are a few things I would like to point out before you consider who you seek advice from and whose advice you trust when it comes to feeding your dog.

Vets: Remember that your vet is not a canine nutritionist. Many vet surgeries are affiliated with a particular ultra-processed pet-food brand, e.g. Royal Canin or Purina. This means they are heavily incentivised to sell you these particular brands. There are some brilliant holistic vets who are doing wonderful things and I'm lucky enough to know some who are changing the lives of so many dogs they work with by doing incredible things with food, supplements and nutrition. These are the people you want on your side when it comes to food, allergies, inflammation, stomach issues, immune issues and itchiness. I work with an incredible vet called Vince McNally who is based in Liverpool, UK, who consults both online or in person, so is available to you wherever you are based in the world.

Pet shops: The advice you get varies so widely. I stood in a large UK chain store recently listening to what a woman was being told when she was looking to purchase food for a new puppy she was getting. The shop assistant told her to avoid fresh or raw food and to focus solely on feeding dry food, as it was 'better for their teeth' and it just saddened me so much. In my opinion, this would be similar to telling an adult that instead of feeding their child fresh meat, vegetables and fruit, it would be better to just feed them crisps and biscuits as it is better for their teeth. My mind just boggles at what we are doing to dogs! Some independent pet shops may stock a larger variety of dog foods and some will even specialise in fresh-food brands. If you can actively seek those out, then hooray as they can offer you advice in person. Otherwise, bear in mind that many big brands will offer training to the sales staff, so their advice isn't necessarily independent and will only be given by the brands they stock in the shop.

Canine nutritionists: These professionals can be incredible, but you need to do your research. Again, many are affiliated with or consult for certain brands, so then they are not independent and will be recommending brands they are paid by. If seeking out a canine nutritionist, check out their history, look at their social media, look at their references and try to find out who they work with to see if you feel they are the right person for you and your dog.

Dog behaviourists and trainers: Then you have people like me, who are not trained in nutrition but have built up huge experience and knowledge by working closely with hundreds of dogs. This is why I won't be recommending a set course of action that suits every dog, as the professionals I work alongside advise on different things according to your puppy and their needs.

However, there is one overarching type of feeding that *all* of the vets and nutritionists I work with agree on, and that is that feeding fresh food is better than feeding ultra-processed kibble. By 'fresh food' I mean meat, fish and vegetables that are either raw or steam-cooked. Dehydrated foods can fall into this category, but fresh is superior.

The more fresh, colourful, unprocessed food we can consume, the bigger the impact on our health. We all know this. Yet with dogs and puppies we are being told to feed them more processed food for health. This just blows my mind and upsets me because our puppies deserve better. What we put in to our puppies impacts their behaviour, their skin, their ears, their paws, their joints, their fur and the way they interact with the world. Let me tell you a story about Ted, my parents' rescue English Bulldog.

When Ted was five years old he was taken to the vets by his previous owner to be put to sleep because of recurring skin problems, ear infections and itchiness. The owner felt they couldn't afford all the medication or the prescription food that the vet had put him on – a hydrolysed fish food that is supposed to be for dogs with skin issues. A vet nurse intervened and fostered Ted, and now we have him.

For his first five days, we kept Ted on the hydrolysed food while he settled in. Then immediately we began to work on single-protein diet testing (see next few pages for how to do this for your own dog), supplementation and figuring out his allergies. After five months we identified the protein Ted could thrive on and identified four others that created allergic reactions. We reduced his steroid intake from five tablets per day to half a tablet every other day. His sores cleared up, he stopped rubbing his ears continuously and no longer scratched himself to the point of bleeding. All from a change in diet! As I write this today, Ted is no longer on any medication for his skin.

I tell you this story to highlight just how much of an impact food and nutrients can have on our puppies and adult dogs. It is never too late to start feeding your puppy or dog well and to the best of your abilities.

We all have different budgets, so seek to do the very best for your dog within your circumstances. Every single little bit helps. So if right now you cannot afford to replace kibble as your dog's primary food, then add in fresh meat, fish, vegetables and fish or olive oils as a topper. Your puppy, just like us, desperately needs the micronutrients within fresh food (steam-cooked or raw) to be able to thrive. Each fresh morsel you add will be powering your dog in so many ways.

Be careful feeding lots of carbohydrates such as rice, potato, sweet potato, wheat and maize, as these ingredients are all fillers. They are cheap ways to bulk out ultra-processed food and not something your puppy requires very much of. Lots of fillers in their food will simply mean your puppy poops heaps more because it passes straight through their system. When a puppy is fed a decent fresh diet, we should see a poo per meal, so if you feed three meals per day, we should see three poos per day. When I meet puppies that are doing four to seven poops per day, that is way too much and a sign there is an issue with what they're eating.

The ideal options to feed your dog would be:

- Raw food you make yourself. There are heaps of nutritionists and companies that will help you formulate your own recipe for your puppy based on their breed, size and output. Don't be tempted to just use a recipe off Pinterest. It needs to be tailored to your dog to ensure you're not missing vital nutrients out.
- Cooked food you have made yourself. Again, you can purchase some brilliant recipes from a holistic vet or canine nutritionist, who can also advise on supplements if necessary.
- Raw food bought from a food company. These packages are usually delivered frozen for easy storage. Do look at the quality of the meat they are using, as they are not all made equal.
- Cooked food from a dog-food company. Again, this usually arrives frozen and you defrost and either feed cold from the fridge or you can reheat it a little if your dog prefers warmer food.
- Dehydrated food. You simply rehydrate this food with warm water and wait for five minutes. It's great for travelling, going to work or anywhere it's difficult to take your fresh food options with you. Also ace for using on rubber lick mats to keep pups amused.

If you take the route of buying fresh food from a dog-food company, I strongly suggest you start out buying just one protein source, such as lamb, chicken, salmon or beef (rather than a variety box which gives you different kinds). Feed just this single protein for two weeks (this means meals *and* all treats from the same protein source), seeing if your puppy has any reactions or aversions to it – see the checklist below. If not, move on to another protein source and repeat. Taking the time to test each protein separately will prevent many issues in the future.

While your puppy is on this single protein, consult this list:

- How does your puppy eat this food? Are they interested in it, OK with it, do they love it or walk away from it? Just like us, puppies and dogs have preferences. Even if they don't have a reaction, if they just don't like a protein it will be obvious.
- What is their poo is like on it? Sloppy, well formed, constipated? Any issues with poo may be a sign that they don't tolerate this protein well.
- Do they start eating grass on this protein? This can indicate gut pain.
- Do you get any bum rubbing or scooting?
- Are they chewing or licking their paws?
- Do you notice any skin changes, e.g. redness, spots, rashes, hair loss?
- Is your puppy doing lots of stretching (more than normal)?
- Is your puppy restless and not sleeping well?
- Is your puppy getting eye or ear issues?

These would be just a few of the things I'd be making a journal or writing notes on. You can take photos of your dog too, as sometimes it is easier to spot things that way. Just don't underestimate what different proteins can do to puppies and how aggravated they can become when on the wrong food or protein. I've seen it time and time again, where the change in diet can transform a puppy or dog, because when we nourish them by providing the right food, our puppies can thrive instead of just surviving.

Lastly, do not feel that your puppy has to eat 'dog food'. Food is food. Food is nourishing, energy providing, delicious, life giving and supportive, and your puppy deserves all of that from their food too. So if people in the park or people around you are telling you that your dog should be fed from a packet designed for dogs, just let it go in one ear and out the other, because you now know better. Food is food, whether you are a human or a dog, and it needs to meet our specific needs but it also needs to be fresh, decent, well produced and as little processed as possible.

HOW OFTEN AND WHEN TO FEED

I suggest that tiny puppies of eight weeks old need to be fed about four times a day. That might be something like 6 a.m./11 a.m./2 p.m./6 p.m. plus, if you feel they need it, an 8 p.m. option. Do bear in mind that the later you feed, the more likely you are to get a poo overnight, so I recommend the last feed is no later than 6 p.m. for our puppies twelve weeks and over, unless you really feel they are hungry or if they are waking up early because they are hungry. Each puppy is different, so do be aware that just because something is working for the littermates in your puppy WhatsApp group it doesn't mean it will work for yours! They each have different digestive systems and getting to know that and understand it is key.

We can start to look at feeding three times per day at around twelve weeks old, so a morning feed, a lunchtime feed and an evening feed. These will vary depending on your own timings and when you get up in the morning. I don't tend to advise feeding as the first thing you do with a puppy, I'd always let them out to the loo first. I would tend to offer the first meal around thirty minutes after your puppy has woken. As above, if you are putting them to bed by 10 p.m., then an ideal feeding time would be 6 p.m. at the latest as we need to leave plenty of time for a poo before bed.

Some puppies, if they are ultra-hungry, if their mother was starved or food was sparse (e.g. a street dog), or if they were fed very poor-quality food by the breeder/rehoming centre/foster carer, might have a higher food drive and we do need to consider that. It can be better to keep them on four meals per day for longer, to keep them satisfied and feeling full. Let them acclimatise and let their body realise that food is now not sparse. Some dogs I work with stay on these meals for life. I worked with a puppy whose mother was a starvation case – at first we had him on six meals per day and even now, as an adult, he is still on four meals per day. His owner has found he is happiest like this, able to function better and less anxious around food, when he is fed on a regular schedule.

Should your puppy work for all their food?

New ideas in dog behaviour and feeding come around all the time, and one that I hear about a lot is that your dog should 'work' for every bit of food. This idea has come from trainers who use a dog's entire food allowance for the day across their training for the day, instead of feeding them two to three meals per day. This argument suggests that dogs should receive food only as a reward for some kind of behaviour, rather than just because it's a mealtime or a treat. I cannot get on board with this. Your puppy deserves to eat their set meals per day. They should not have to graft, perform or follow rules just be fed. Eating isn't a 'nice to have' for dogs or people, it is a fundamental requirement of life. So making our puppies and dogs work for every morsel has no place in my methods and ways that I train dogs.

Will my puppy put on weight if I give them lots of treats?

I use treats in all of my training and behavioural work and this is in addition to their actual meals that they need for growth, energy and development. If we are feeding natural, lean, decent treats there is far less worry about dogs putting on weight because of treat usage than if we are using kibble, processed treats, treats full of wheat, soya and meat meal. Eating those processed treats will of course pile on the weight, as they contain ingredients that dogs don't need in their diet. When you are considering how to use food, treats and rewards, know that your puppy can still eat meals and you can still use treats and food as rewards. It's not one or the other.

UPSET STOMACHS

One of the most common things I see with new puppies and then puppies at differing times in their lives is a stomach upset, and then the vet recommending that the puppy be put on a 'hypoallergenic food' for the rest of their life. The puppy starts on the journey of being branded a dog with 'stomach issues' and it becomes impossible to get them off that food without more upset reactions. I want to help you and reassure you that there are other ways to manage a sensitive stomach.

The reason hypoallergenic kibble doesn't provoke a reaction in a puppy or dog is because there is barely anything in there that nourishes, provides nutrients or helps a dog thrive. It's not so much that the food is 'solving' the issue of the sensitive stomach but that there are usually so few nutrients for the dog to react against. If you were eating cardboard you wouldn't likely have an allergic reaction to it, but it wouldn't be doing you any actual good!

You have multiple options when it comes to a puppy with a sensitive stomach. We just have to go about it carefully and with consideration. Our overarching aim should always be to get our puppies eating a decent fresh diet. Whether it is a brand you buy and have delivered or one you make, the choice is yours, but there are always options.

I have managed this myself with our dog Pip. When we took him on at seven years old, his stomach issues really were tricky. It took me around eighteen months to get him sorted, onto an even keel, but we got there. In the first two months of taking him on, we nearly lost him to pancreatitis due to stress, plus his stomach has always been incredibly sensitive, so with the combination of emotions, stress and sensitivity, it would mean regular bouts of diarrhoea and upset stomachs. We have done a great deal of gut repair using supplements and have found a lean, fresh diet that really suits him; he scoffs the food, it is highly nutrient dense and it keeps his poo firm. Sometimes it can take a bit of trial and error, but you'll get there.

If your puppy has been fine and then suddenly gets an upset stomach, provided they are drinking water, are not lethargic and are not exhibiting any other symptoms, then you don't need to panic. You can cut out a meal and instead feed them a bone broth to provide the electrolytes and nourishment to support their gut. Like us, puppies can get an upset stomach because of stress, emotions or environmental input, e.g. being in a new, busy place. It isn't always down to food, so don't be tempted to rush into changing their diet immediately just because their stomach has been a bit upset.

If you feel stress or anxiety is impacting your puppy and their stomach (which is much more common than people realise) then we really need to look at how we support this, alleviate what we can and add supplementation to aid the body with processing the stress, as well as the impact it can have on the body, so that it doesn't move into adulthood with them. I strongly believe in gut supplements that can help to repair and support the gut – this is worth considering if you have had a puppy who has suffered trauma, stress, hasn't had the best start, has had to take antibiotics or is struggling with frequent upset stomachs. There are of course varying kinds of supplements and I would suggest chatting to a canine nutritionist, as they tend to have better options than the ones in the tube from the vets.

If the stomach issue is down to an illness, gastrointestinal bug, infection, etc., then of course these need to be treated by your vet. But what we do after the immediate bug has cleared is then a big deal, as if they're given antibiotics, pain relief or medical treatments of any kind, this can wipe out the gut microbiome or greatly impact it at least.

We cannot overestimate the impact of medication in puppyhood on behaviour when they grow into adult dogs. Do not be tempted to just leave it and assume it will all be OK. We now know that, within humans, our gut–brain axis is clearly linked and impacts our hormones, the way we feel, how we interact with the world and much more. The exact same thing is true of our puppies and dogs. We need to make sure that the food we are feeding them is replenishing our puppies and we may need to look at adding in a gut supplementation. These can range from actual moor muds from Germany that are highly nutrient dense, to capsules we can sprinkle that will help guard against further issues, to amazing remedies and liquid tinctures that we add to fresh food. What is used and suggested would depend on what your puppy was going through.

You should remember that your puppy doesn't need to have an actual vomiting bug or diarrhoea to have stomach issues. If your puppy is licking or chewing their paws or keeps stretching their body out, then it can indicate that they may be struggling with their gut – keep an eye out for these early warning signs. This is why I recommend starting your puppy on single-protein diets so you can be aware of any reactions as early as possible and be ahead of the game.

Recipes for recovery

BONE BROTH

I use a slow cooker to make bone broth for dogs, but you can also use a pan on the hob. The main thing is that it needs to be on for at least eight hours.

INGREDIENTS:
Leftover bones – I tend to use the chicken carcass from a roast dinner. You can use raw bones you buy from the butcher (beef, chicken, turkey, lamb)
Apple cider vinegar – two tablespoons
Leftover vegetables that you want to use up, e.g. carrots, celery

METHOD:
—Place the bones and vegetables in the slow-cooker pot/ saucepan and fill the pot with water so that the bones are nearly covered.
—Add two tablespoons of apple cider vinegar to the water. Bring to the boil, then lower to a very slow simmer for eight hours.
—Leave it to cool.
—Once it's cooled down, sieve the pot into a new container and throw away the bones, veg, etc., making sure there are no shards, bones or pieces in the liquid you keep.

—Decant the liquid into a jug and store in the fridge to use, or you can pour into ice cubes and freeze them to defrost when needed.

—If there is a fatty jelly, don't chuck it away as this is great for your dog so long as they don't suffer from pancreatitis. Just feed a little at a time or add to the cube trays to freeze.

—Ideally, feed bone broth at room temperature when your dog needs a boost, is recovering or when they are off their food. You can use this broth in the summer to rehydrate your puppy or give them broth ice cubes to chew on to ease teething pain. So many amazing uses for such a cheap but incredibly effective recipe!

Recovery meals

Ideally, after a period of illness, you would just return your dog to the fresh food you normally feed them, as there should be no reason to adjust it. You can make it more liquid-based by adding more warm bone broth if you think they need it.

The old advice was to feed a recovering dog on chicken and rice. However, chicken is a common allergen for dogs and rice is a grain which passes straight through your dog's digestive system. These days, most people don't recommend that if your dog has been unwell. If you're looking for a gentle recovery meal, I recommend a recipe which vet Dr Nicole Rous suggests, composed of 50/50 cooked pumpkin and cooked turkey. Pumpkin can soothe the gut and is easy to digest, and turkey is not a common allergen like chicken.

If your dog is usually on a raw-fed fresh diet, you can still feed them raw food but you may just want to use plain mince (supermarket is fine) to reintroduce it, and add some bone broth to it for a couple of days. Then transition them back onto the normal fresh raw diet you either make or buy.

If you feed dehydrated, you can just rehydrate the food with your bone broth for a few days until they seem back to normal.

You don't need to be making huge changes to a dog's diet when it's been unwell: you just support them with minor changes and get them back onto their usual food. I tend to avoid the tinned or dried food that vets offer as the ingredients are highly processed. Giving turkey and pumpkin, or just a raw protein with broth, is far superior and more nourishing.

ALLERGIES

Now this is a gigantic topic because allergies can come in many different formats, but here are some of the most common ways we can tell that a puppy or dog is struggling with an allergy:

- Itchy ears.
- Inflammation – could be one or all of: skin, eyes, ears, paws, fur, redness, spots.
- Infections – ears most commonly, weeping eyes, rubbing face and ears continually.
- Chewing of paws – chewing the digits, paw pads, licking.

- Scooting of bottom – rubbing of bottom area frequently.
- Needing to itch or rub themselves – you will find puppies on their back rubbing on carpets and along walls, sofas, chairs, anything with texture or fabric to get a good rub against.
- Disturbance in sleep patterns – may sleep in a tight, curled-up position a lot.
- Short fuse, snappy, grouchy – just as you would be if you were uncomfortable!

Ideally we want to begin working on figuring out the allergy immediately rather than waiting to see if it resolves itself. Before dosing your puppy up with antibiotics or allergy-suppressant drugs, I would highly recommend you first try single-protein diets to figure out where the inflammation and reaction is coming from; I work very closely with a vet on this.

If a puppy has been bred poorly – had a poor diet, poor environment or high stress load – it isn't really a wonder that they are going to be struggling with issues that emerge in the form of allergies. For some of our other dogs, we have to look at the reality of what breeding is doing to allergies. Many breeds struggle because either breeders continue to breed from dogs with inflammation and/or allergies, or they are breeding for particular colours with disregard to health. Here are some examples:

- West Highland Terriers are renowned for allergy issues. This shouldn't be the case. We can actually eliminate this if we are actively not breeding from dogs with issues.

- Blue Staffies have huge issues with allergies, reactivity and gastro issues because they are being bred for the blue gene, not for health.
- I'm seeing French and English Bulldogs with big allergy issues all the time because, once again, they aren't being bred for health but for looks.

Your choice of a certain breed or colour can end up costing you thousands more pounds in veterinary fees, specialist assistance via nutritionists, holistic vets, behaviourists and trainers. This really is something to bear in mind.

Recently I've found that many clients have been advised by their vet to do a food-elimination diet but in a way that won't actually help them ascertain what is causing their dog an issue. Many are being advised to use a kibble as a base and to use different proteins on top to trial, but this simply will not work. This is because using a kibble that has many, many ingredients and is so highly processed will not give us a reliable indicator on what is causing an issue. We need to not use kibble of any kind: it has to be fresh (cooked or raw) meat on its own, otherwise it is not a single-protein diet test. And that includes treats: we cannot be feeding cooked chicken as an elimination diet and then give all sorts of other things as treats. That will greatly impact what you are seeing, so any treat would need to just be the cooked chicken too. It really has to be that simple, and for a minimum of ten days per protein.

Lastly, there are brilliant advances on supplementations that we can provide our puppies with and that we can continue feeding into adulthood, sometimes for their entire lives. The efficacy of these depends on the quality and the format, though, and they need to be highly targeted and personalised for your puppy. Avoid social-media adverts telling you that by feeding this one supplement in a treat format your dog's anxiety or reactivity will just disappear: that is not true! Supplements will be a part of our 'whole dog' approach and are needed as support, but they will not solve everything if that is the only thing you do! I can't give specific recommendations on supplements as every dog's need will be different, but I would recommend working with a holistic vet or canine nutritionist who can create a plan with you.

TEACHING MANNERS AROUND FOOD

There are many ways we can start to teach our puppies about how we want them to behave around food e.g. to not grab, not beg and not steal croissants from kids' hands!

The main thing is to make sure that your puppy is satisfied with the food they are being fed at home – that means their food is fresh, nourishing and not a dry food like kibble or tinned wet food. Any dog fed unsatisfying food is bound to go searching for better options in life, and who can blame them?

Taking as our starting point that our puppy is well fed on satisfying and nourishing food, we can begin to think about various ways we can teach our puppies to behave around the temptations of human food. Here are some easy and simple ways to begin this process . . .

- Don't feed directly from the table while humans are eating. Instead, put a bowl in the middle of the table and place in it any scraps or leftovers you want to give the puppy. After the meal, use these scraps as you see fit, e.g. add them to treat-dispensing toys or their usual feeding bowl, or use for training.

- Start using a particular mat that you bring out at meal-times, and reward your puppy every time they go on to it. This mat can be a memory-foam bath mat or similar. It sounds simple, but this will take weeks of work, and you can encourage this by giving a chew on it or rubber lick mat that they begin to associate using when only on that mat. You can begin your training by simply throwing a treat onto the mat for your puppy to pick it up. While they are stood on it, you can keep dropping treats onto the mat. Then start to wait for them to offer you other behaviours that are desirable, like choosing to do a 'sit' or a 'down' with you continuing to reward by dropping a treat between their toes.

- Don't take your puppy to a pub or café when they are really hungry. Sounds obvious, but a hungry dog is going to be a pain, in the same way a hungry child is! Either take food with you to feed them or take a chew that they can eat.

- If you don't want your puppy around the kitchen/dining table at all, then from the first day you need to have your baby gate up at the kitchen or dining-room door and use it. Reward your puppy for being on the other side. Again, you can use a mat and provide something for them to be eating or chewing, e.g. a raw bone.

- If you have young children in highchairs, be aware that they are capable of creating a begging dog in a matter of hours by hand-feeding from their chair without you even realising! My two-year-old did this with Fred the Great Dane, who could rest his entire head on the table next to her! It took begging to another level.

- Make sure you are feeding a variety of fruit, veg, fish, meat, bones, chews and scraps to create variety in your dog's diet, unless you have been advised otherwise because of allergies. Rest assured that feeding a dog your food scraps does not increase their interest in human food. Food is food as far as a dog is concerned!

- If you want to eat out with your puppy in restaurants and pubs, you need to start working on teaching them to get used to being on a lead when you are carrying drinks. You can practise this in the kitchen. It is the same for them being attached by a lead to a chair or table leg: start work on this at home. You can't expect them to lie calmly on a lead under a table in a busy environment like a pub if you haven't shown them how to do this in their own spaces. Slowly build up to more distracting places.

- If your dog enjoys their crate and they are tired, there is no issue with you putting them in the crate while you eat.

- If you are struggling with your puppy being a land shark in the evenings when you just want to sit and eat something, feel free to use a movable fence, which tends to be metal grid panels that fix together but are easily adjustable. Sounds strange, but you can put it around your table or by your sofa to section off the room. Just make sure your puppy can still clearly see and hear you, and that you have left plenty of chewy things on the other side of the fence for them to play with.

- If your puppy is small enough, you can use their puppy bag placed by your feet. Unzip the top part so you can reach in, but leave the sides shut so they can't get out. This keeps them safe and will stop strangers' hands from bothering the puppy, but also allows you to drop in the occasional scrap or treat to reward your puppy for staying still.

CHAPTER SEVEN

Your Puppy Resting

Resting can feel like something that vanishes from your life when you get a puppy! Focusing on rest and sleep will reward an owner, as a rested puppy will bite less, be less boisterous and will be much more biddable and open to training and learning. So all in all, establishing a strong routine around rest and sleep is a key thing to master in your puppy's life.

SLEEPING

Here are some very approximate guidelines on how long I would expect your puppy to be awake for, before needing to go to sleep and nap . . .

- Eight weeks: thirty to forty minutes.
- Ten weeks: forty-five minutes to an hour.
- Twelve weeks: an hour to an hour and a quarter.
- Sixteen weeks: an hour and a half.
- Six months: two and a half hours.

Sleep is the time when your puppy grows, repairs, recuperates and processes what they have learned and experienced.

If your puppy is twelve weeks old, I'd be looking at them being awake for forty-five minutes to an hour, and then getting them into their pen or confined area or simply sitting down and doing your own thing. Begin to establish a routine that signals to your puppy that it is time to wind down and get ready to nap; there are cuddly toys that can help with this as they have heartbeats that soothe your puppy, and you can add one to their bed when it's time for a nap, then remove it when you want them to wake up.

You cannot simply stimulate a puppy and keep them up for their full time limit and then expect them to just flip a switch and go to sleep! That definitely won't happen. We have to provide what I call 'a bridge' to get our puppies to be able to sleep.

First ensure your puppy has been out to the toilet, as you don't want their sleep to be interrupted. Then, as we approach a puppy's sleep time, instead of playing or training we need to be calming things down, providing spaces and places to rest, things to mouth on and soft toys to lay against to encourage sleeping. This is when you would move the stimulating toys out of reach and swap in the teddy bear, the yak chew, the tea towel with a treat wrapped in it, the toilet roll to shred. If your puppy can't get on the sofa, it's a good idea to simply sit on the sofa with your legs up, out of reach of your puppy, or at the table doing work. Allow your puppy to roam but provide lots of places to rest – blankets, rugs, beds, jumpers. Let them have access to the items I described but don't interact with any of these toys. Allow your puppy to get a bit bored and go and lie down and chew and go to sleep.

If you use a puppy pen, then this would be when you put the puppy inside the pen near you and swap the items within it to be restful. Then you'd work nearby, watch TV or make a cup of tea, so they know you are around and nearby for reassurance. You can even sit next to the pen and work on your laptop or phone.

I have no issue with puppies falling asleep on your lap, so long as they aren't biting you and hurting you. If your puppy likes sleeping on you, that is fine for a nap or two a day, but do make sure you set up other areas for them to be able to rest too. For example, while you watch TV their cosy bed could be by your feet, or buy a heated mat (you can pick them up very cheaply on the likes of Amazon for around £14) and put a blanket over the top so that your puppy feels cosy. However, do also bear in mind that the way your puppy slept with their litter will impact how they sleep with you. I always actively look out for this when I'm observing litters for clients or helping them choose a puppy. You cannot expect the puppy who slept with all the other puppies on top of them to simply stop seeking that physical contact now, just because they no longer live with their littermates. They don't realise that! So make sure you are realistic about your expectations and what your puppy is able to do.

CRATES

In the USA, crates are a much bigger phenomenon than in the UK. Crates are used to contain puppies and keep them out of the way. In the most extreme cases a crate is used to contain the puppy at all times unless they are being walked, going to the loo, eating or being trained. Some people believe that puppies should not be allowed to free roam or be out of their crate as it will create bad behaviour. I strongly disagree with this idea. If we don't allow our puppies to explore and be independent, how do we expect them to learn how to live alongside us in the human world?

In my opinion, we should let our puppies free roam, be independent, explore, be curious, build resilience, learn about their environment. But in order to do that, we must have puppy-proofed that environment. A crate restricts the puppy from the environment, instead of making a situation safe for them. If you ask me, that's the wrong way around.

Now, if you want to use a crate for your puppy to sleep in, that is absolutely fine, but do bear in mind that many, many puppies I work with do not like crates and do not want to be in them. I won't spend my time forcing them to accept a crate if they don't enjoy it. And I think there are far better ways to spend your time!

If your breeder crate-trained your puppy with their mother and litter from day one, you will stand a good chance of your puppy enjoying this type of set-up. But you will need to ask specific questions as to how that crate was used. Many breeders may describe their puppies as 'crate-trained' when in fact they mean they slept in the crate with siblings with the door open and inside a bigger pen. That is not the same as a puppy learning to sleep in a crate alone with the door shut!

Once again, if you choose a puppy from a breeder who uses the Puppy Culture method, they will have done consistent work on creating great associations with each of their puppies using a crate in a kind and considered way. Many rescue puppies will be unhappy in crates, after having to travel in them without proper introduction or training.

If you want to use a crate for your puppy, I tend to advise that either the crate is by your side of the bed (right next to it so you can put your fingers through to reassure the puppy). Or, if you are sleeping on the sofa, then the crate is right next to that. I do not believe in using a crate to put a puppy in a room all alone and letting them cry it out or expecting them to be fine overnight alone. We want to be working on teaching secure attachments where your puppy doesn't feel stressed or traumatised or abandoned.

If you are using a crate, you do need to make sure that it has enough space for your puppy to turn around in and to be able to sleep fully stretched out. They should have a mattress inside, and have a bumper around the sides so that the puppy is cosy and there are no draughts. I would also fill the crate with soft toys for your puppy to nestle into and snuggle against at bedtime for comfort.

Your puppy may fidget about as it gets comfortable in the crate – if it's not settling, you can simply place your hand nearby so that they can smell you, see you and touch you. Once settled, they will let you know if they need the loo because they will start whining or knocking on the crate. Then you can pick them up and take them straight outside to go to the loo. This is likely to happen several times a night when your puppy is small. Some puppies may then not want to go back in the crate once they have come out. So you then have to decide whether you want to spend your time at 2.30 a.m. settling them, waiting for them to drop off and soothing them, or whether you would prefer to just go back to sleep and let them choose where they sleep, e.g. in the crate, on a bed beside the sofa or on a blanket on the floor. That has to be your choice, but the hassle of toilet training at night is, in my experience, one of the main reasons people stop using crates.

What if my puppy doesn't like crates?

If you don't want to use a crate or your puppy just hates it, don't panic. Don't feel like you have failed. You have not. Your puppy, like many puppies before it, just doesn't want to be in a box, and that is fine! You might find your puppy is fine in the crate with the door open – you can then leave the crate in a pen so that the puppy isn't able to run all over the house. Or just have a bed and a folded-up blanket in the pen, so the puppy has a few options of where to sleep. You can also have a dog bed beside your bed with a fence around it so that the puppy is right next to you but can't wander round the whole room.

Additionally, you can have the puppy in the bed with you, which, in my opinion, is not the huge issue that everyone makes it out to be. Puppies are social animals, designed to be with littermates. You are its companion now, so of course it wants to be close to you. Do not panic if your puppy will only settle in the bed with you at first. You can train them out of this slowly by having a dog bed on your bed, so that you put the puppy in their bed on your bed, and slowly move it down the bed and eventually off the bed and beside it. Nothing is for ever!

I think new owners get very caught up in what others will think and how they will be judged. But I'd ask you to remember that sleep is critical for all of us – that applies to you as well as to your puppy. Some puppies nail a solo sleep routine quicker than others, while others need more contact. There are no hard and fast rules. We do what feels right at that time with that puppy (which may differ with your next dog). Adapt, adjust and stay patient.

WHAT TO DO IF YOUR PUPPY WON'T SLEEP

Ooof, it can feel exhausting when a puppy fights sleep! So first off, take a deep breath and know that there are several things we can do to help.

Firstly, go back to the advice on food (page 193). If you are feeding your puppy too many carbohydrates or food like kibble, dry food or tinned foods, then you may be creating extra energy by giving them too many carbs and sugars. Try changing their diet to fresh food to see if this improves the behaviour.

We need to look at your puppy's schedule for the day. Are you exercising them enough? Are you doing all your outings in the morning so that by the evening they are ready to cause mayhem? Have their walks been interesting and varied, or were they just dragged around the block? Have they been played with enough, and mentally stimulated?

You may need to address your balance between providing mental stimulation and tasks with your exercise outlets. By this, I mean that our pups need an active combination of walks, adventures, training, mental stimulation and being taught. Figuring out the right combination for your puppy can take time, as what a Working Cocker Spaniel needs will be very different from a Shih Tzu. Our puppies are clever beings that need to use their brains as well as their legs. Achieving that balance can take some time to figure out, especially as they get older and are able to do more, so do factor that in too. That perhaps they have grown, aged and matured and you haven't considered that part of their daily schedule.

It might be time to think about the play you are providing. If you are constantly playing high-energy, full-throttle games like ball lobbing, tugger or chase games, then you might be lighting a flame that won't be easily dampened just because it's bedtime. We cannot stoke a puppy up and then expect them to just settle because we now want them to. Think about slowing things down in the evening, removing overstimulating toys, providing a chew for your puppy to work out some energy and release calming hormones ready for sleep.

Lastly, consider your breed or crossbreed and genetics. If you have taken on a working dog, a dog designed to be on the go for hours, you can't then be angry at them for displaying this kind of behaviour. If you have selected a puppy that has incredible energy, abilities and durability, then it is going to be down to you to facilitate pottering opportunities (garden), training opportunities (mental stimulation) and decent and proper exercise (walks), and you may need to consider putting your dog away by itself when it is sleep time. Many working breeds cannot just send themselves to sleep, as we have bred them to be 'on' all the time. So to turn them off often requires a crate, a pen, a fenced area or a space where they can chew and rest quietly.

DEALING WITH SLEEP
DISRUPTIONS AND REGRESSIONS

It is a fact of puppyhood that your puppy is going to have setbacks when it comes to sleep. These can come in the form of suddenly waking in the night even after your puppy has been sleeping through it for ages. Or the setback can be the result of a disruption in routine or environment that unsettles them during a developmental period.

I find that ten to twelve months can bring up sensitive times for our puppies and sleep. As owners we are lulled into thinking we have it sorted at this point, and then something as minor as an outside noise, a fox in the garden or a mouse in the kitchen can wreak havoc because our puppy loses their confidence.

The main thing to remember is that a sleep regression is 'usual' with puppies (just as it is with human babies), so don't feel alone or like you've made a mistake. What we do have to bear in mind is that usually at these points and phases our puppies are looking for one thing – reassurance. And if we provide this, the sleep disruption will tend to dissipate and resolve itself as they grow.

We can provide reassurance for our puppies in various ways when they're struggling to sleep. It may be that you bring them into the bedroom, or perhaps let them sleep in the hallway outside the bedroom door, or in a spare room next to your room. This allows them to hear you, smell you and feel reassured that you are close. They should be toilet-trained by now, so you should not be worrying about them weeing and pooing overnight.

You may also find that your puppy needs a change of bed as it gets older, because being physically bigger may mean that they need more support or to rest differently. Experimenting with bed options can pay dividends for a dog that isn't sleeping well. For example, if you have a bigger-breed dog, e.g. a Labrador and upwards, then you may need to invest in a more supportive bed with sides for it to lean on, or one that is bigger and allows stretching out. These simple changes can make a big difference. Think about providing a duvet for a dog who likes to snuggle or dig themselves into their bed. Settling your puppy is about observing what your dog favours and implementing it.

Do also bear in mind that our puppies are going to be starting to be impacted by hormonal influences at this age, and the changes that these bring can be gigantic. The hormonal impact can start to have a bearing on sleep, behaviour, eating habits and more. This may be a good time to start thinking about hormonal supplementation to support your puppy.

CHAPTER EIGHT

Your Puppy and Saying No

My aim as a dog behaviourist is always to set a puppy up to succeed so that it doesn't constantly hear a barrage of 'No!' or 'Leave!' However, we do still have to be ready to stop our puppies carrying out some behaviours, without denting their confidence or making them anxious about new situations.

Wherever possible, we should think ahead about how to avoid issues (like not leaving a tempting plate of ham on a low table and then shouting at the puppy for helping itself). However, on some days everything goes pear-shaped despite your best efforts. The meeting runs late, the school run goes wrong, the lasagne ends up on the kitchen floor. Life doesn't always go according to plan, so we need to have systems in place to let our puppy know that, even in trying circumstances, biting your face or attacking your ankles isn't tolerated.

When your puppy is doing something you do not want, your first aim is to walk away from it if you can. Don't respond to the behaviour, don't shout 'no', just calmly remove yourself from the situation. That would be our ideal option, if it is safe to do so, as it removes us, gives us a breather and allows your puppy's behaviour to be disrupted so that they can calm down. This isn't just for puppies – I sometimes have to do this with my kids and just silently scream into the fridge so they can't see me ready to implode. Don't feel guilty: life is hard, raising a puppy is hard, and like I said, life is not a perfect set of circumstances. That is just the reality.

If we can't walk away entirely, then we can at least step over a baby gate and stand behind it so that our feral puppy can't leap at us, grab us, lunge at us or touch us! Again, if you know they are overtired, overstimulated, the house is too busy, the walk was too much and your dog is struggling, you need to remember this moment and learn from it for the next time. But in the actual moment, getting yourself over the other side of a baby gate is the next best thing. And you can sit on that side and throw little treats for your puppy to go off and sniff, to help calm them down. Or poke some cold veg from the fridge through the bars for them to sink their gnashers into: anything that gets them off your skin, jeans, toes or ankles.

If you are really struggling with mouthing and your puppy is now a big puppy, e.g. ten months plus, and this behaviour shows no signs of abating, it may be time to consult a professional. Your puppy's adult teeth should be in place and their need to teethe should have dissipated. At this age I would still expect mouthing on the lead, picking up stuff and needing to chew, but mouthing on people, biting and needing to chew constantly may indicate some other stuff is going on that we need to get to the bottom of. A great place to start is to have their teeth formation checked out by a vet.

Lastly, it is OK to say no to your puppy. Or a version of that! I tend to use a noise as a disrupter instead: something I can make with my voice that isn't used at any other time. People often feel like the advice to only reward good behaviour means never saying no, but for me, the reality is there are some times when you need to stop a behaviour immediately.

If my two-year-old was banging me over the head with a saucepan, I would not be able to just calmly wait for them to stop before rewarding a different behaviour. The same is true with a puppy or dog. If they are hurting you or you feel upset and anxious because of something they are doing, you are allowed to let them know. I don't mean by shouting or hitting, I mean by disrupting the behaviour and then giving them something else to do.

A good example of this is when I was working with a slow-to-mature Doberman Labrador cross who was, at sixteen months, still very much a puppy. He just wanted to play but he was massive and in his version of 'playing' he got hold of my coat and arm and basically rolled me onto the ground. There was no malice intended – for him it was an incredible game – but it was not one that I wanted him to think was repeatable! So I hooked the handle of his lead over the prong of a nearby fence, restricting his movement. This stopped the game so that I could get up. When I went back over and he tried to repeat the game, I just stepped back so that he couldn't take action as he was restricted by the lead. After a couple of attempts, he realised that this game wasn't happening and he chose to do something else, which I rewarded immediately. I then picked up the lead and we started playing the new game with heavy rewards to show this was a good idea. It's always worth looking at *why* they are displaying this behaviour, and you may need to reassess their schedule, food, play and exercise (e.g. amount of each).

'LEAVE IT'

Puppies are close to the ground, and the ground is often a source of all kinds of intriguing nuggets of food. Teaching a 'leave it' command is very helpful, and the sooner you start to teach this the better. Do bear in mind that your puppy is going to be picking stuff up in their mouth left, right and centre because they don't have fingers that can explore for them. It is hard but you will need to work on not just grabbing things out of your puppy's mouth. Instead, you should focus on letting them explore the world and rewarding them when they drop the item, by giving them a little treat.

I've taught thousands of puppies to leave items and my favourite way is as follows:

- Hold a low value (non-exciting) treat in one hand and clench your fist closed, so the treat can't be accessed.
- Allow your dog to sniff your hand (they may start to paw, lick or nibble it, but ignore all of this and wait!).
- As soon as they remove their attention from your hand (they look away, sniff the floor, step back) immediately verbally praise them, and put a treat on the floor for them to take.

- Repeat this a few times.
- Start to add in your cue word when they remove their attention, e.g. 'leave it'.
- Then, when you put the treat on the floor, start adding your cue word for taking it, e.g. 'take it'.

We can then build on this technique in other situations and scenarios, but the reason this works so beautifully is because it is about the puppy deciding to remove their attention, and you capturing that and rewarding it. Remember, do make sure to reward from the floor and not your hand – that is key!

Years ago, when I was first learning about dogs, I was taught that you teach a 'leave it' command by offering some food and then yanking the lead to exert a quick pull back on the dog's neck and collar. Although thankfully few behaviourists teach this method any more, I still see it recommended, especially on social media. Please understand that yanking and pulling your dog around by the neck may teach it to leave something, but it will have two unwanted side effects. The first is that this kind of aggressive yanking will negatively impact your dog's developing skeletal and muscular system. The second is that it will make your dog wary and distrustful of you.

If you are looking to teach things like 'leave it', there are so many other ways than just placing a piece of food down and yanking your dog away by their throat. What we need to understand is that for a puppy to truly learn what 'leave it' means we need to have worked on the technique I outlined above, rewarding the puppy when it ignores the food. Then we build on this as follows:

- Teach them about this command in the comfort of their own home with a treat that isn't too exciting.
- Repeat in other areas of your home.
- Repeat with other distractions.
- Repeat outside with the same dull treat.
- Repeat outside with dull treat plus distractions.
- Then we need to start the whole system again for teaching them to leave the next type of treat/foodstuff and go through the whole process of teaching the cue, rewarding the response and then proofing it in other locations and with other distractions.

It is totally unfair to teach a 'leave it' command to your puppy inside with a piece of dry biscuit and then expect them to understand that this same command applies to an extremely exciting chicken bone on the street.

In addition, simply yanking your dog away isn't actually teaching them to leave the item, it is teaching them to stay away from food when on the lead or else they will feel pain. That is only one very particular set of circumstances, it certainly isn't generalised and it won't keep them away from food when they're off the lead.

HOW TO SET BOUNDARIES

The main reason puppies encounter issues around boundaries is because of inconsistency in the way they are trained. Establishing clear boundaries for your puppy means having clear conversations with your partner, children, family members and anyone who spends time with your puppy about what is acceptable behaviour and what isn't. This applies to behaviour from the puppy and behaviour from humans, it's not just one way!

For example, if there are two of you who live with the puppy and one of you lets them on the sofa and the other doesn't, then this is very hard for the puppy to figure out. They are going to end up really annoying the owner who doesn't want them on the sofa, which will affect the relationship between the dog and that person. Whereas if the pair of owners decide to let the puppy onto the sofa, then they can set up an area where the puppy is allowed and collaboratively work together on training the puppy where to lay and how to get up and down safely. The whole experience becomes so much more rewarding for both owners and for the puppy to learn, and expectations on both sides are clear.

Puppies like understanding boundaries and thrive when they understand the rules – whether that is how to play tugger or to wait before going out of the front door. It is worth just sitting down and thinking about what the behaviours are that you want to invest your time and efforts into. This will depend on your personal circumstances, and shouldn't be led by what you've seen on social media. For instance, I see owners spend so much time trying to train their puppy to sit by the side of the road before crossing. This is hard to do, and something you rarely use with an adult dog. Instead, I'd say you would be better to simply train a 'wait' and release cue and put your efforts into teaching incredible eye contact. Both of those will pay dividends later in lots of different environments.

One thing I will say about boundaries is don't believe that if you stop your puppy going on the bed or sofa or upstairs that they will be better behaved. This kind of thing does not impact their personality, and it doesn't make them dominant or confused about 'hierarchy' in the home. It is up to you to work according to the best of your puppy's personality and funnel your energies into rewarding the things you want your puppy to keep doing instead of getting caught up in the negative and focusing on the continual challenges. There will always be challenges, but if you have researched your breed and puppy well, you will be set up for those anyway.

The only time I suggest you are strict with boundaries is if you have a puppy that is guarding things like a sofa or a bed or items they have found. In those cases, then we do have to be very careful not to inadvertently reinforce these habits. If our puppy is struggling with guarding, then we would not be allowing them onto the bed or onto the sofa as removing them can create a battle that is best avoided. So use baby gates, fences and house lines to keep your dog away from the places it's guarding, and ensure you aren't manhandling the puppy, dragging it off a sofa or bed, or constantly worrying where it has gone.

WHAT TO DO WHEN IT GOES WRONG

Even the best owner, and the best puppy, will have off days. Things go wrong, and it's important not to beat yourself up but to remind yourself that the only thing we can do is to learn from our mistakes. What we learn will depend on what went wrong, but here are some of the most common issues I hear from my clients, and the solutions I advise:

The one where your puppy runs off into other dogs and doesn't bother listening:

This is what your 5-metre long line and harness were designed for, so use these for the time being rather than letting your dog run free. Really think about the situations you are putting your puppy into and whether they are too distracting for your puppy's current level of recall. You may need to rotate your days in terms of where you walk, going from quiet one day to a little more busy on another day. We cannot expect your puppy's full concentration at all times, but we can set them up to succeed by walking in places to suit their distraction abilities. We can also think about finding friends to walk with who have calm older dogs that you can walk alongside and reward your puppy constantly for walking next to you. Hard work, but it will be worth it when it pays off in the end.

The one where you take your puppy and kids out on a walk and you are left screaming into a tree:

Trying to keep an eye on a puppy and kids and other dogs can be too much. If you've had a walk like this, just accept it was a lot to take on. Next time, walk them separately or have an extra pair of hands to help. Or if you have to take both kids and dog out because you have no choice, then I'd suggest driving somewhere so your baby or child can fall asleep in the car seat and you can get to a quiet spot, sit next to the car to keep an eye on your sleeping baby and put your puppy on a 10-metre long line. Then lob treats into the long grass while you sip a hot coffee from the flask you brought with you. Can you tell I've done this before?! Sometimes we just need to make life super simple for ourselves. As when we remove the stress from ourselves, we remove it from our dogs.

The one where your puppy won't settle when you have friends over:

Visitors can be very exciting for a puppy, and it's easy for them to get overstimulated and start biting or running around madly. If this happens, make a plan that next time you will walk your puppy before your friends come over. Then, when your friends arrive, do a short walk around the block together before they come in the house so that your puppy gets used to them. When you get back home, give your puppy a chew or treat-dispensing toy and keep refilling it to keep them occupied while you make a cup of tea. And when you sit down with your friends, you can keep the puppy behind their baby gate with their toy, chew or bone. Make sure that the visit isn't too long so that you aren't sitting there anxious and worried. Set yourself up to succeed by letting your friends know that their visit will just be 30 minutes long until your puppy is a little older and less likely to get overwhelmed.

I hope these examples demonstrate that we can learn from each mistake or thing that goes wrong and make changes for the next time. We and our puppies are constantly learning. And if you take anything from this section, it should be that the environment we place our puppies in heavily impacts their ability to listen, learn, focus and respond.

Remember my motto: if the environment is difficult, ask less of yourself and your dog to make it easier.

CHAPTER NINE

Your Puppy and Learning About the World

Puppies are curious little beings and the more they get to safely explore as tiny puppies, the more resilient they become. What is important from the early days is that we provide our puppies with safe opportunities to explore and investigate, without any shocks or trauma. This allows them to feel confident and comfortable in being independent and discovering the world. Everything in this section is something I would encourage you commit to throughout your puppy's young life, even up to the age of three years if you have a big breed that matures later. Keeping your puppy's confidence and curiosity high is something that will pay off for its entire life.

STARTING TO EXPLORE

It is tempting to wrap an eight-week-old puppy in cotton wool and confine them to one space in the home for safety, as well as to stop them toileting everywhere. I actually find that heavily confining a new puppy tends to work against you and can end up creating dependence and over-excitement at new spaces. But if we've thoroughly puppy-proofed our home (see page 72), then we have nothing to worry about when it comes to letting a puppy roam around the home. Wee and poo can be wiped up and cleaned. Lack of confidence isn't so easy to get rid of.

Alongside puppy preparation, we should make our environments safe for pups to go and walk around and play in by making sure the spaces aren't risky or full of items they can chew or swallow. Let your puppy roam without following it from room to room. This will create well-adjusted, curious puppies who can figure things out themselves. If you feel unsure, you can put pet cameras in each room so that you can monitor their actions on your phone. As part of puppy-proofing I would of course put baby gates up around steps and stairs, and if you have rooms you cannot puppy-proof then you will need to put a baby gate up to stop them having access. But if you want your puppy to learn to settle in different rooms, on differing levels of the house, you cannot simply confine them to the kitchen and then let them loose upstairs on the rugs at ten months of age. You won't have shown them what to do, how to be or how to interact with that room, and ten months will have passed with them not having had access to spaces within your home. We have to be prepared that our puppy will pull at, dig at, wee on, chew on and run around a room, so prepping it for this is what we focus our time and attention on.

TOYS

There are a gazillion options available when it comes to puppy toys, and between them my clients have bought most of them. Yet something I often see when I visit a home with a new puppy is a pile of toys that are pretty much untouched. And that's because the toys were bought before the owner understood how the puppy likes to play. They've bought balls for dogs that don't like fetch, or tugger toys for dogs that are more interested in chasing. So while it's tempting to buy toys in preparation for your puppy's arrival, I'd refer back to the 'before you bring your puppy home' section and restrain yourself to just those recommendations.

When your puppy has arrived home, you will begin to see what motivates them, and this will give you more of a clue as to what kind of toys you should get (refer back to pages 88–91 for more on motivation).

Whatever toys you end up buying, my suggestion is that you should divide those toys into three sets.

Set 1: These are toys that you allow free access to. The puppy can play with these whenever they want.

Set 2: Interactive set. These are restricted toys which you bring out to use, give and play with. They are only used for interactive play between you and the puppy, and are put away once that play session is over.

Set 3: For the park. These toys only come into action outside the house, which makes them all the more exciting, and this novelty will really help with recall and distraction while you're out and about with your puppy.

PREVENTING RESOURCE GUARDING

There are many ways that we can work on preventing resource guarding, and I've outlined the main ones I come across with my clients.

Ask your breeder the right questions

The first is to make sure that the puppy we are buying does not come from a mother or father who resource guards. That sounds so obvious, but you would be amazed how little this is discussed with breeders when selecting a dog. You should ask specific questions of the breeder and listen for any hints of any issue. You can ask questions such as: are the puppies fed out of the same bowl or are they fed separately? (Ideally we want puppies not squabbling for food from birth.) Have the puppies had access to lots of different resources? (For example, toys, chews, bones, random items. Take a look around too as that should help you figure it out according to what you see the puppies interacting with and what they have access to.) You should also observe this when you visit the breeder to meet the puppies and ask about how the adults are fed, about play time, about toys, treats and so on.

Feeding all the puppies from the same bowl immediately creates competition between puppies for a resource of which there is a limited amount. Instead, we want to see that there are more bowls than there are puppies, and plenty of food to go round. If you had a litter of six puppies, I'd want to see at least eight or nine bowls or plates of food around and spaced out so that the puppies have space but also their own portions and an ability to get more if they need it. If the idea that food is scarce and needs to be fought for or guarded is imprinted from your puppy's primary socialisation in the litter, it will forever be a battle. This kind of very early influence on behaviour around food is not something you will be able to 'cure' but something you will instead have to manage.

Be cautious about day care and other competitive situations

Assuming your puppy has not come to you with resource-guarding issues, you can prevent these problems developing by being very cautious about placing your puppy in any situation where it has to compete for attention, treats, meals, toys or time. That means (as I've outlined before) a busy day care is not a great place for a puppy. These kinds of hectic competitive environments and repetitive experiences can trigger a dog. I have had so many clients where resource guarding has begun in their puppy after just one week in a day care setting, because the puppy has felt panicked repeatedly, multiple times a day. The repetition reinforces the puppy's need to defend itself and its food/toys/carer.

Keep your puppy well nourished

The other way we can prevent resource guarding over food is by making sure we are feeding a brilliant, fresh, nourishing diet. A well-nourished puppy doesn't try to eat everything because it won't be desperate for nutrients. See page 193 for information on how to best feed your puppy.

Don't pull things out of your puppy's mouth

We've mentioned this before, but something I see often is a puppy who has developed resource-guarding issues because its owners keep pulling things out of its mouth. Puppies love to explore with their mouths and aren't necessarily going to eat everything they pick up. It's very common for a puppy to pick something up, mouth it, and then drop it. But instead of waiting to see if this happens, owners panic, wrestle the puppy and plunge their fingers down its throat. This is so intrusive and shocking to the puppy, and no wonder they have a reaction to it.

First things first, as a new puppy owner you should always have a pocket or small bag of tiny treats with you, as they are the quickest way to distract your dog. If you fear that your puppy is going to swallow something dangerous, stay calm and keep your voice at a sing-song playful pitch while dropping lots of tiny treats on the floor. This will usually motivate your puppy to start hoovering up the treats, and it will naturally drop whatever was in its mouth. You can then create a path of treats for your puppy to follow, leaving the object behind. Try not to simply grab the object the moment it's dropped, as that can teach a puppy that if they drop something, you are going to take it away. All these early experiences really matter.

And of course the best way to ensure your puppy doesn't pick up things that it shouldn't is to plan ahead and puppy-proof as much as possible.

Try an exploration floor

Giving your puppy a chance to mouth and explore different objects in a safe setting is an outlet for their curiosity, and this helps to curb resource-guarding tendencies. A puppy who knows it will regularly be offered lots of exciting things to pick up, mouth and chew is less likely to guard or hoard anything. As always, set your puppy up to succeed.

Go around the house with a box and collect random objects that you don't care about, which pose no threat to your puppy and that you won't need to be worried about them chewing or swallowing. Here are some examples:

- Loo rolls.
- Reusable coffee cup with no lid.
- Old socks.
- Old towel.
- Brown paper bag.
- Toothpaste box.
- Pieces of rope.
- An old book.
- Fruit and veg, whole or cut into pieces.
- An old cricket pad.

- An old cricket ball.
- A bucket.

Each day, you are going to place three to five objects on the floor and let your puppy explore them, pick them up, chew on them, drag them around and gnaw at them. Crucially, while your puppy does this you will ignore them and get on with something else (knowing your puppy is safe as you have chosen these objects carefully). If they bring something to you, of course you can praise them for this. Don't take the object from your puppy or touch it, just praise and pet the puppy.

These kinds of tasks are very important for building confidence and independence in your puppy. Ensure you always have safe items on the floor that your puppy is allowed free access to and that you praise it for using. And ensure you don't grapple anything from their mouth, even if it is to play with. We want to be constantly working on teaching our puppies that sharing is a great thing.

Food bowls

Never take a food bowl away from a puppy or a dog while it is eating. You can add items to a food bowl while your puppy is using it, but never take anything away. Ensure your puppy is being fed in areas where they don't feel threatened by other pets or kids. I used to feed my Great Dane in our garden, as he was huge and it meant he had more room. That meant I didn't need to worry about the kids mistakenly bashing into him and making him feel threatened. All of us deserve to eat quietly, calmly and without interruption – the same is true of our puppies and dogs.

SURFACES

This is something that is super-simple to introduce to pups but will pay dividends later on. If we teach our puppies to not worry about differing surfaces, it can make travelling, walking and interacting with the world so much easier. Our puppies are highly tactile and sensitive creatures, their paws and pads are how they feel the world – this sounds obvious but as owners we tend to give so little thought to it.

As mentioned before, on page 88, at eight weeks old we can start to introduce differing surfaces to puppies, in so many small but fun ways, so that it becomes part of our training and isn't something for them to feel fearful of. Here are a few ideas that you can very easily incorporate into your puppy's life. If you have an older puppy and haven't done this, there is still time. However, just bear in mind that they may feel more worried or take more time and that is fine. If they are scared or worried, please stop.

- Buy some large tiles from a cheap tile shop and use treats to train your puppy to walk across them slowly.
- Buy a strip of carpet to practise teaching 'down' and 'sit' on.
- Lay pieces of paper or card stuck together into a line on the floor and put treats on them for your puppy to hoover up and walk along.

- Buy a whiteboard and lay it down and teach your puppy to walk across it and sit on it with treats.
- Open up a cardboard box, lay it flat and poke holes using a skewer. Insert treats into the poked holes and let your puppy stand on, drag and rip to get the treats out. (Also great for tiring an energetic puppy out of any age.)
- Cover some books in tin foil and teach your puppy to step onto and then down from them, using treats.

CHAPTER TEN

Your Puppy Being Handled

I've come to realise that many issues around our dogs biting, nipping and growling stem from the way that we as humans handle and invade their space when they are young. Puppies are adorable and appealing, and we often expect them to accept our advances, boundary-pushing and overzealous contact when we wouldn't be able to tolerate the same treatment for ourselves or our children. I can't imagine that anyone would, without asking, pick up a stranger's child, or wake up their sleeping baby, or smoosh their toddler's face – yet these things, and more, happen to puppies all the time.

We can help our puppies with boundaries firstly by protecting them and making sure that they have their personal space respected. We can also work on teaching our puppies what gentle handling can look and feel like. We can do this by teaching our puppies hand targeting, e.g. where you teach your puppy to touch the palm of your hand to get a treat. We can teach our puppies that if they want a lift down the stairs (especially useful for smaller breeds) that you sit on the top step and let them walk onto your lap, then pick them up and walk down the stairs – instead of just grabbing them. I recommend this for breeds like Dachshunds who are very good at getting up the stairs but then get stuck!

AT THE VETS

Even if your puppy has no requirement to go to the vet, if your vet surgery is nearby, it is worth popping in once a week when your puppy is small. Let your puppy go in, be fed a treat, be touched and 'examined' (even by a receptionist – you don't need an actual appointment) and come back out again. This way you are building positive/ neutral associations with the vets for your puppy.

On top of this, we can begin to teach our puppies some handy things that can help with examinations. At home we can teach our puppy to touch the palm of our hand with their nose and get a treat as a way to teach them to stand still. We can work on consent handling by starting to slowly and carefully examine an area of their body. If they choose to walk away or turn their head or disengage from the interaction, it's essential that we respect this, and stop touching them. And if they choose to stay and come back to it then we can re-engage.

We can make examinations part of a game, e.g. using a lick mat while you examine toes. You can check an ear, then chuck a treat, and repeat. The key is that we begin getting your puppy used to being handled and examined early in life, and we create the expectation that this will be a pleasant experience.

Do not allow your vet to take your puppy away from you to be given vaccinations or examinations or medications. You need to be present to see how they are being handled and what they are having done to them, to ensure that your puppy's associations with the vets remain positive.

AT THE GROOMERS

I advise all of my clients when they look for groomers to seek out individuals who do grooming either from their home or, if they use a space, they only do one dog at a time. Avoid any groomer who has multiple dogs on the premises at once, and especially those who operate a day care from the salon at the same time. You would be surprised how many do this, as it is an extra income stream. However, this kind of environment is noisy and full of other dogs, while your puppy is being handled by a stranger. It's an overwhelming situation for most puppies and even grown dogs, and isn't a situation I'd encourage or recommend. So many puppies begin to have behavioural issues after their first visit to a groomer, so it is really worth going through in detail how you do not want your puppy forced to go through an entire hair cut if they are hating it. I would always suggest that the first couple of visits are kept simple. So, for example, for a Cocker Spaniel:

Visit 1: Little meet and greet to the venue to meet the groomer, no grooming.

Visit 2: A trim on ears, around eyes, paws, around the back legs/bottom.

249

Visit 3: A bath and towel dry.

Visit 4: Bath, trim as above, and dry.

Ideally you would space this out over the course of a month with one a week so that in a short period your puppy builds a great association, and the next time they go for a proper groom in a few months, their association is firmly cemented.

On page 102 I introduced you to the idea of how you might start using a soft baby brush on your puppy. Doing this as early as possible begins to get your puppy used to the concept of being handled in a gentle, no-stress way. So let's ensure we continue that throughout its grooming experiences.

Here is an example of how you can begin to introduce a bath:

WEEK ONE

Place a rubber bathmat in the bath (so the puppy doesn't slip and get scared of the bath), and smear some peanut butter on the side of the bath. Pop your puppy onto the bathmat in the bath, and let it lick the peanut butter from the side. Practise this each day for a week for just two to three minutes each time (no water in the bath yet).

WEEK TWO

Repeat as above but with 1cm of warm water in the bath. You can run the water before you lift your puppy into the bath.

WEEK THREE

Repeat as week one, but with 3cm of warm water for each day that week.

WEEK FOUR

Repeat as week one, with 5cm of warm water and a warm flannel gently wiped over their fur for each day that week.

If your puppy is tiny, you can use the kitchen sink to make it less scary. You should build up the process really gradually until you are at a point where you can shower or bathe your dog happily depending on what they prefer. Some dogs will happily hop into a walk-in shower if you go with them, so it can be worth trying out a few options to see what your puppy prefers. For example, for Ted we use a bowl of warm water and a cloth to clean his paws and legs after walks, as he much prefers this to a hose or shower. (In the summer he absolutely loves playing with the hose, so we use it to wash him secretly, but he thinks it's all part of a game!)

You may be thinking that this seems like a crazily long time to teach your puppy to have a bath, but it shows you how much time we must invest in introducing new and strange concepts slowly and carefully and with the boundaries the puppy shows they are happy with. Dunking your new puppy into a sink or bath full of water straight away might feel faster in the short term, but you could be creating problems around trust, handling and grooming for the rest of your dog's life.

If you have a breed that doesn't shed very much, such as a Cockapoo, you need to be aware that their unshed fur has a tendency to mat. And if matted hair is left too long, it becomes impossible to brush out the mats, and it will need to be shaved off. So when you bring your puppy home, introduce a puppy brush, a soft one that you pair with one of you brushing while one of you feeds treats. Do not force them: if they walk away, let them. Do not pull at mats and knots in your puppy's fur. Instead I'd prefer that you just cut these out quickly and easily with sharp hairdressing scissors so that we don't create a negative association for your puppy that being brushed means fur pulling and pain. We want it to be as pleasurable as possible.

Think carefully about the items you use to groom your puppy. I advise you not to use those hard metal brushes with bobbles on the end. These get stuck in hair and pull fur, and many dogs hate them. Also be careful about grooming tools that profess to do things in half the time: often they will actually damage the coat or pull at it and the hair won't ever grow back the same way, which is especially important when we have puppies with double coats, such as Border Terriers.

In short, grooming is about the long game, and it will reward your investment of time and patience. Lastly, do not take your puppy to a groomer where there are lots of dogs floating about as this is hugely stressful. We want a calm and chilled atmosphere, not frantic, noisy and distressing.

BEING PICKED UP

Obviously you won't have as many issues with your dog being picked up if you have a large breed. Issues around being picked up are understandably more common with our smaller breeds like Mini Dachshunds, Cavapoos, Border Terriers and Jack Russells. If your puppy asks to be moved, picked up or to get on your lap, I have no issue with it, whatever size it is, provided you won't break your back lifting it. But my rule of thumb tends to be if your puppy isn't actively asking to be picked up, don't pick them up!

The one exception to this rule is on the stairs, and particularly with Dachshunds. Many Daxies can get up the stairs but can't come down them as their long backs make this difficult. In that situation what I tend to do, rather than pick the puppy up straight away, is go and sit on top step. I wait for the puppy to choose to get onto my lap themselves and only then do I carry them down. Giving the puppy the choice is the key.

When we have tiny puppies, it is so tempting to prevent them doing something by just picking them up and taking them away from the situation. As a behaviourist I urge you to avoid this. At first your puppy may just be a little bewildered by being lifted into the air, but you may start to see that your puppy begins to nip you, turns and tries to bite or gets a bit growly and grumbly. If you ask me, these are all acceptable behaviours when someone has, without warning, grabbed you by the underside of your stomach and lifted you off the ground! Instead, we need to go back to the section on interrupting behaviours we don't want and use those techniques instead of simply picking them up and causing issues.

CHILDREN HANDLING PUPPIES

This leads me onto children and their handling of dogs. The age and experience of the child will of course impact the way they handle the puppy. But it is important that children are not allowed to pick a puppy up unless the puppy is asking for it. Children must not be allowed to hold the puppy like a baby or to restrict the puppy from moving. We should also avoid children thinking it is OK to follow a dog around, and instead encourage them to sit on the floor and allow the puppy to come to them. If a dog has got down from the sofa where the child has sat and moved away from the child, the child must not be allowed to follow, as the puppy is clearly signalling that it needs space.

A walk away or disconnection is the first subtle sign that the puppy wants space from the child. If we don't teach our children to respect this, we may end up with difficult reactions from your puppy further down the line, like growling, nipping and biting. So please don't risk developing these behaviours. If necessary, use baby gates so that your puppy can be left alone and have time away from noisy, prying hands.

When you are out and about and other people's children want to pet your dog, first of all see if your puppy wants this interaction. Do they avoid the child, do they walk away, are they not the least bit interested? In that case, you just say no. If your dog is interested in engaging, then a great way of controlling that contact is for you to drop several small treats on the floor for your puppy to hoover up, then allow the child to gently pet from a situation where the puppy can see their hands. I'd avoid encouraging kids to give the treats or else we can get puppies who jump up because kids don't reward quick enough. Then the children start shrieking and the puppy gets excited and jumps and nips. So set it up to succeed! Interactions between puppies and children work best if you direct how you want it to go based on what your puppy shows you. If the puppy was interested at first but then chooses to walk off, don't bring them back and don't try to lure them back with treats. They have clearly shown you that they have had enough and that is to be respected.

CHAPTER ELEVEN

Your Puppy Playing and Making Friends

When we take on a puppy we have all these expectations of how we'll train them to be a certain way, and then as we pay attention to our pup it slowly starts to dawn on us that they have their own personality, likes, dislikes and desires. These personality traits and preferences can really impact the way our puppy experiences the world. Again this is why your breed, breeder and puppy selection matters. If you got your puppy from a rescue, you choosing a puppy based on highly detailed information, with your questions being answered and relevant information being passed on to you will be key. Every experience your puppy has had in its short life will impact how they interact with potential new friends – whether they be other dogs, children, adults or other animals.

Let me give you some examples from my clients . . .

I had a couple who bought a Border Collie called Dinah, who was born into a home where the breeder lived alone in a remote farmhouse with no family and no visitors. The mother of the litter was very nervous, and by the time the puppies were picked up by their new owners at eight weeks of age they had only ever encountered two humans – their breeder and a vet. These puppies had no positive or neutral associations with humans that they didn't know, and this is a problem when we look at what we want our puppies to associate with people – that they equal good things. These puppies were severely lacking in this. Not only were these puppies coming from a dog with a nervous, anxious disposition but in their primary socialisation period they had only ever met one person for a very brief spell (apart from their breeder) so they had no positive associations with visitors, people outside of the home, in the car or on the street. The combination of all of these components meant that Dinah was petrified of everything, extremely anxious, did not enjoy meeting humans and could not cope with people coming into the home. When you are thinking that breeding and breeding experience doesn't matter, it really does.

The second example I wanted to tell you about was when I was helping a client seek out a rescue dog. The client had been through a demanding time and needed a dog that would easily transition into their home. The dog had to be great with people and other animals to ensure the owner could cope and thrive. I found a great little scruffy terrier mix through a rescue organisation I know well. They are located abroad, so we couldn't visit the dog. Instead, we spent a number of weeks with me submitting questions and asking them to send me videos in response. I asked questions based on what I could observe, like seeing how the dog interacted with people, out on a walk, and how it was interacting with other dogs in the compound playing. I would go through each video and observe the body language, the interactions and the behaviours and then go back with more feedback and more questions before we agreed to bring him over to foster. These details matter as it enabled me to prepare my client, set him and the dog up to succeed and still to this day he sends me the most amazing photos and videos of them together loving life. They are a match made in heaven.

I tell you these differing stories as it is important how we breed, raise, select and identity the puppy or dog that we will come to share our home with. And the expectations we put on them.

MAKING FRIENDS WITH PEOPLE

Assuming that your puppy already has a positive association with people, we are going to build on that, slowly but surely. The key is to let your puppy show you who they want to interact with and take it from there. Some people may be wearing something your puppy is unsure of, so it may take them time to sit and observe the person in the hooded puffer coat or the man in the high-vis jacket across the road. The important thing is that we let them watch and learn and see that nothing bad happens.

We can actually help our puppies form some of these positive associations with new people. For instance, we can pick up clothes from charity shops or jumble sales. Don't wash these clothes, just lay them out on the floor and allow your puppy to explore, climb over and sniff them. This allows slow exploration of new-people smells at home in a space that they feel safe in. You could introduce a different item each day for a week or two during their secondary socialisation. And then donate the items back to the charity shop (after you've washed them to get rid of any puppy contributions). It is a win–win situation for all of you.

If you have family members who live far away, but with whom you'd like your puppy to form a happy association in their early weeks, don't despair. Send a toy you know your puppy will enjoy to your relative. Ask them to keep the toy in their house for a week and play with it, handle it, tuck it under their arm while they watch TV every night, and basically get their scent all over it. Then have your relative place the toy in a ziplock bag and post it to you. When your puppy is given this toy to play with, that person's scent has been introduced in a formative period with happy associations. There are so many little things we can do that can create a big impact.

With people coming to your house to visit, it is worth remembering that they need to equal neutral or positive outcomes for your puppy. The last thing you want is lots of adults and kids coming over, grabbing, picking up, following and manhandling a puppy. This risks creating the perfect storm for a dog, who starts to react to people coming to the house. They predict that people coming is going to equal having their boundaries breached, which is less than ideal. Considering your dog's feelings is important and really paying attention to what your dog wants to do when people are over is key.

The ideal starting point for this is to think of your puppy as an adult dog, and what you would like them to be doing when they are five years old and a visitor arrives. Then we work backwards.

If you would like your puppy to wait in the kitchen while you answer the door, that is where you begin. You could initially use a baby gate so that your puppy could see where you were going – although for some puppies that are excitable personalities or breeds, this could actually make it harder!

You would then make sure you throw treats down on the floor for your puppy to sniffle and snuffle out while you answer the door. Then if it is the delivery person, they never need to worry about them, but if it's someone coming into the house to visit or stay, your puppy would now be busy with treat-snuffling, which, as you walk into the room, you could continue by throwing more down for them to carry on with. Let your friend sit down and then give them a toy on a long rope to play with your puppy – so that we encourage play and a connection that doesn't involve over-handling, picking up or jumping up. We set our puppy up to succeed. You can then intervene and give your puppy a chew so that they take it to their bed or simply lay on the floor and crack on with it alone. This then means your puppy can be left alone and not touched while you have a cup of tea or coffee. In this process we have taught our puppy:

- There is no need to go to the front door.
- Good people come in and puppy can carry on eating treats (but not given by the visitor).
- The visitor sits and plays, but in a non-confrontational way.
- The puppy gets to go and chew and process any feelings into the chew, and is allowed to relax alone.

If your puppy then wants to climb onto laps or receive contact, then let them show you! Your guest can sit on the floor and you can let your puppy come to them. Do not allow visitors (adults or kids) to go and pick the puppy up and do not pick the puppy up yourself and pass it to the visitor. That isn't a trustworthy interaction from your puppy's point of view – as they had no say in it and we don't want them to start to distrust your contact with them.

If you have a puppy that you feel is worried about people, wees themself when people make contact, shies away and doesn't want to be touched, please respect this and try to not push them. Pushing them to be confident and interactive isn't a long-lasting training programme. Instead they need time to watch (from behind a baby gate with people at a distance), for visitors to leave them alone and not be overbearing, and for you to provide treat-dispensing toys and chews behind the baby gate so they can be kept busy. We should not be allowing worried dogs to go to the front door as that fear will simply build in a busy hallway with people pushing past, bags coming in and out, hands grabbing them and a high level of noise. It certainly won't enable them to build confidence by simply being immersed and pushed into it.

If your puppy really loves people and you are finding it hard to stop them jumping up and saying hi to everyone, consider it an excellent issue to have. Honestly, many owners with anxious dogs would be thrilled to have this problem. As an owner, we want to ensure your puppy carries on adoring people and forming great associations with them. All we might want to work on is rewarding the puppy for staying close to you until the point when you give permission for them to greet someone new.

Teaching your puppy to be OK around children

Children are either exciting or worrying for a puppy. They can be exciting because they often smell of food, are high pitched and run about, but they can also be scary for the same reasons, as they are unpredictable, shouty, scream and often lack boundaries. So if we keep these main things in mind, we can teach our puppy some good associations around children. The main thing is to make sure you do not try to do too much and actually end up causing problems because you have allowed your puppy to be put in too many situations that create scary or negative associations. With that in mind, in no particular order, here are my top-ten tips for creating a happy association between children and your dog:

- Meet children on neutral territory where there is heaps of room, e.g. a park instead of places like a pub, house or kitchen. Then the puppy can be on their long line and get away, and children can be distracted with doing something else. Do not allow kids to chase the puppy.
- If your puppy walks away, gets up and moves, or turns their head away as a child approaches, then stop the child interacting or allow your dog to walk off and be left alone. If we taught this to every human being, we would greatly reduce our bite statistics.
- If your dog is interested in children, build up great relationships by keeping them at a slight distance to avoid over-handling – some great ways of doing this are asking kids to go and hide the dog's ball

around the house or in a pile of leaves in the garden, so the puppy can go off and search for it. If your dog is mouthy, you can buy a cuddly toy and tie a really long piece of ribbon around the toy's neck e.g. 2 metres long. Then the child can hold one end and walk along trailing the toy so that the puppy can focus on the toy and it keeps the child's hands well out of the way. You can also tie a long line around the toy so that the dog can either teethe on the long line or the toy. Anything is better than kids' hands.

- If you have a child that can follow directions, then give the child a cup of treats and let them ask the dog to sit. As soon as it does, get them to drop a treat to the floor. Get the child to walk away and let the puppy follow, ask the puppy to sit and drop a treat on the floor. Repeat and repeat and repeat. This gives the child and the puppy a purpose, it rewards manners (bum on ground) and it stops the puppy from jumping for the treat as it is dropped to the ground, not given from the hand. If you want to help your puppy, you can actually spend a couple of days teaching your puppy this game, so that when they play it with the child, they already have an idea of the rules. Do make sure you are stood close by, so that if the child is delayed getting the treat from the cup, you drop one instead, to make sure the reward is given promptly and properly.
- Remember that children misread dog body language all the time. You always need to be the 'blocker' so that you can be sat or stood in the middle, between the dog and child. That means the dog is protected but

also you can stop the child if they go to do something that you or the dog won't like, e.g. to grab.

- Use baby gates and movable fences. Prevent, prevent, prevent any problems arising. Everyone thinks it won't happen to them, but I have many clients whose adult dogs now despise children due to things that happened in puppyhood, and now those adult dogs will go to bite and some have bitten children. Some of the things that happened have included children chasing a puppy, children throwing toys at a puppy's body and head, a child pushing Lego into a puppy's ear, children crawling under a table to get to a puppy when it was already worried, or running around the house screaming and puppy couldn't get out of the way quick enough, and children who keep grabbing the puppy from behind. And many more things. So if we use baby gates and fences, it means you can prevent these things when the puppy is tired, the child isn't listening, or the kids have friends over and the puppy isn't safe to be around them because they are having a crazy moment, or you need to just take your eyes off puppy and child, so making sure they are separate means you minimise your risks.
- Do not be tempted to go and hang out at the school gates or school pick-up time as a way to teach your puppy about kids, it is more likely to backfire than be useful. The last thing you want is huge groups of screaming kids running up to your puppy with no escape route. Instead, you could stand in the park opposite a school at play time, so the kids are behind fences (!) and you are at a big distance (e.g. 10 metres

away) and you can let your puppy watch and observe, and when they disconnect you can reward them with a treat or playtime. We are just trying to teach them that all the noise and movement isn't anything to be concerned about without risk of it backfiring.

- Don't take your puppy to spaces and places where you will have very little control over interactions, such as pubs or playgrounds. You heavily risk poor associations being formed, for instance, children invading spaces, with nowhere for the puppy to escape, and this then becomes overwhelming. If you want to teach them about the pub, go when the kids are at school!

- Do not allow kids to grab things from your puppy's mouth, even if it is their favourite toy, action figure, car or teddy bear. We need to be understanding that our puppy is also a baby and is exploring the world and figuring it out by putting it in their mouth. Revisit the section about avoiding resource guarding and apply this, or at the very least, in the heat of the moment, calmly walk away and 'drop' a more interesting item on the floor that you know your puppy will jump up and grab, e.g. a toilet-roll tube, a cardboard coffee cup, a plastic bottle, an old jumper, anything that your puppy will go to and grab and that you can happily let them chew for a bit.

- Prevent over-handling and touching. No grabbing from behind, no picking up, no children shoving their face in the puppy's face, no waking them up, no climbing into their bed or touching them when they eat. These are so basic but so crucial. I once had a very famous client ask me to help them 'make' their puppy be OK with their son putting it into a headlock. Instead, I spent my one-and-a-half-hour session going through in great detail why this wasn't possible, would never be OK and explaining that if they didn't start putting boundaries in, their child would be bitten in the face. These boundaries could stop your puppy turning into an adult dog that bites children. All of us should want that.

MAKING FRIENDS WITH OTHER PUPPIES

Despite what Disney movies might have us believe, it's not a goal for our puppy to have a gazillion friends! Rather than besties, what we want for our puppy when it comes to other puppies is a happy interaction or an interaction that is neutral. Don't underestimate neutral when it comes to puppies and dogs. A puppy or dog who isn't that bothered is always preferable to one who is overexcited and unpredictable.

If you have a friend or know people in the park with other puppies or young dogs, do not be tempted to just stand around and let them run riot together. I know it is tempting and makes for tired puppies that will sleep heavily when you return home, but this rough and tumble runs the risk of creating associations that can create long-term problems.

Let me give you an example. I often see puppy owners standing together drinking a coffee and comparing notes, letting the puppies circle each other, play and chase. There is usually one puppy who is more persistent or pushy than another and let's say your puppy ends up being chased by the pushy one. Your puppy may be running not for fun, but because they are anxious. This only needs to happen a couple of times with that particular puppy, in that particular park, with you, and your puppy will begin to create negative associations with the puppy, the place and your ability to protect it. These associations then materialise or become evident as our puppy ages and starts to either retaliate when chased, become more independent or seek you out less because you weren't helping them out the first few times it happened.

I don't use this example to make you feel guilty but more to help you understand that where you take your puppy, who and what they socialise with, and how those interactions go, impacts your puppy and the adult dog you end up with.

With a new puppy, I advise you to be very wary of comments made by other people in the park such as 'they're just playing' or 'let them sort it out themselves'. It's your job to protect your puppy from being chased, frightened and ultimately affected long-term by unsupervised play.

As a dog behaviourist, people often come to me with puppies who were permitted to play continuously or were not removed, helped or protected when a situation with other puppies or young dogs became too much. You wouldn't leave your child to keep playing with another child who kept hitting or poking them in the eye, so let's not do that for our dogs either.

The tricky thing is that 'too much' varies for each puppy. We also have to be careful about 'allowing' behaviours. A classic one I see is the Whippet owner who thinks it is OK for her puppy to chase every dog or puppy they see, because they are bred to chase. However, if you let your puppy or dog behave like that, you will come up against issues later on – as your dog will think that 'chasing' is the only way to interact with other dogs, and not all dogs will want this. We have to consider the implications of teaching a dog born to chase that chasing is allowed everywhere and anywhere. That then becomes their reaction to everything and you will find it very hard to control them. Whereas if we have a Whippet puppy, from the early days we should instead teach them:

- To wait before they can chase the toy.
- To wait and then be released with a cue before they can chase the ball.
- To play with puppies and dogs of other breeds in ways that aren't just chasing.
- To work heavily on their eye contact training. I call this focus work and it is greatly underestimated for all puppies.

And we need to understand that our Whippet pups can find a busy environment extremely tiring, as everything that moves can stimulate them. So thinking about where we walk, where we train and where we do things is incredibly important.

If we were to contrast this with a French Bulldog who plays in a very different way, it can be very physical: body barging, pushing, rough-and-tumble type play. If Frenchies are only doing this sort of play and are allowed to just run at and body slam every dog they meet, it also won't end well. This is why we have to think about what we permit, encourage and allow when our puppies are young, as it impacts their future interactions.

This list isn't exhaustive, but it should serve as a way to help you think and consider your individual puppy, their breed, what they are designed to do, areas of strength, things that may be challenging and how you are going to begin to work on these from the day you bring your puppy home.

MAKING FRIENDS WITH ADULT DOGS

Calm older dogs can be some of the best learning partners for a puppy, as long as they are patient and playful. What we don't want to do is try to force an interaction with a senior dog who has zero interest in frolicking with a puppy. That will just result in the poor senior dog being annoyed and then having to tell the puppy off. We want to avoid this for the sake of both dogs. It is not the older dog's job to keep reprimanding the puppy – you need to be involved and prevent your puppy from being a nuisance. That might be in the form of using a harness and long line to keep your puppy at a distance where they can watch and observe the older dog but they cannot bombard it. Or actively working hard on parallel walking outside with heaps of treats to distract your pup from the older dog, and then a romp in the long grass to get rid of some energy after concentrating so hard.

If introducing your puppy to older dogs, we want to be looking for walking pals who are steady, can listen to their owner, are happy to sniff and be independent but every now and then like a little play. These kinds of dogs mean your puppy can do some great 'social learning'. As well as interacting with the senior dog, your puppy will watch and gauge how that older dog interacts with other dogs and people. So choose your companions carefully, as your puppy is absorbing everything from the company they keep.

It is critical to think about this if you are bringing a puppy into a home with an existing adult dog. If your adult dog has behavioural issues (e.g. reactivity or aggression) then you will need to be factoring in huge chunks of time to exercise your puppy on their own, teaching them the ways you want them to interact with others, without the influence of your older dog. If you allow them to just follow and learn from the adult dog, you may be doubling your workload as you'll end up with two reactive dogs that are now impossible to walk. In that situation I'd ask if bringing a puppy into the home is the wisest thing to do. You would likely do better to focus your funds, time and efforts into your existing dog before bringing an impressionable puppy into the household.

MAKING FRIENDS AT DOGGY DAY CARE

One of the biggest issues I see for puppies and adult dogs is puppies being placed in day care and with dog walkers when they are simply too young and not ready for the demands of this environment. And sadly the majority of those facilities are not set up to take the time and to work through all of the points above about play, chasing, appropriate behaviour between puppies and adult dogs, etc. Instead they will probably match dogs up by size or age, and, while of course it's sensible not to mix up a tiny little dog with a huge boisterous puppy, there is so much more to consider. It's not just puppies that develop issues in day care. I have worked with adult dogs who have become reactive to puppies because the day care saw they were tolerant so put them in with the puppies and 'used' them as the nurse or nanny dog. That adult dog reaches a point where they aren't tolerant any more, as they are sick of being chewed, tormented, jumped on and humped, and eventually (and understandably) they begin to snap. This is not fair on the adult dog at all, and it's not the fault of the puppies either as they aren't being restricted from bothering the older dog. For this reason and many others, as unpopular as it may sound, I reiterate that my advice is not to use doggy day care or a dog walker until your dog is around two years of age.

ADVOCATING FOR YOUR PUPPY

Advocating for your puppy means taking charge of a situation and stepping in to ensure your puppy is not overwhelmed, overstimulated, intimidated or harmed. This is the opposite of just leaving dogs to it, as I believe responsible dog ownership is about firstly setting your dog up to succeed by not placing it in challenging situations or, if you find yourself in a challenging situation, taking action to get your dog out of it.

Advocating for your dog can mean many things to different people and different dogs. I offer below some ways that you can advocate for your puppy. Many of these methods are easy to employ but have the potential to change your dog's life for the better for ever. That may sound dramatic but it is true. We often get caught up in focusing on the big stuff, such as teaching them toilet training or sleeping through the night, and forget about addressing the many little unsettling incidents which make up our dogs' lives. The reality is that the cumulative effect of these multiple difficult incidents can be far more significant to your dog in the long run than the after-effects of one big incident. So I'm here to help you focus on the little things for your puppy, as addressing the little things early can prevent major problems later.

How to advocate for your puppy around other dogs:

- If your puppy is not enjoying being chased, grab the other dog by the harness or collar and pass him to their owner. Then either pick up your puppy or put them on their lead and move away.
- If another dog is barking at your puppy and you can see your puppy doesn't like it (their ears are back, their tail is dipped and their back hunched), then walk over, put your dog on their lead and walk away.
- If your puppy is jumping up at your legs to be removed from a situation, pick them up or put their lead on and walk away.

- If you are walking with your puppy on the street and other dogs approach, put your puppy on the inside of the pavement, closest to the wall, so that you can be the blocker between them and another dog passing. Do not allow your puppy to greet every dog on the street, and do not allow other dogs to approach your puppy on the street.
- Don't allow other dogs to run into and up to your dog. Try to block the other dog with your legs or, if they are being persistent and annoying and their owner is nowhere in sight, put the other dog on your lead and walk them over to their owner and return them.
- Just because another owner tells you 'it's fine, it's just play' doesn't mean they are right. Trust your instincts, as your puppy being harassed by their over-zealous puppy or dog is not fine.
- When you see other dogs walking towards you on the street, provide space, cross over, allow room, don't make them cross paths if there isn't room or you can see the other dog is lunging or pulling. You are simply allowing your puppy to avoid an intimidating situation. You would do the same for your child!
- Do not expect to just take your puppy into another dog's home and for it all to be fine. I suggest meeting first on neutral territory such as a park or field, and then initially separating the dogs in the home with baby gates. Set your dog up to succeed by planning this carefully, and keeping fully on top of the situation, not simply hoping for the best.

How to advocate for your puppy around people:

- Block unwanted interactions by standing in front of your puppy. Put your puppy behind your legs and drop small treats on the floor for them to sniff out.
- Tell people your puppy has fleas if you don't want them to be touched!
- If you and your puppy are in a room with children (including your own), always be your dog's blocker, positioning yourself between your puppy and the child so that unwanted contact can be stopped. This will prevent accidents like a child tripping over or landing on the puppy.
- Teach every human you know that when a puppy or dog gets up and moves away, walks off or disconnects from them, they *do not* follow. Moving away is your puppy's first sign of trying to create space by removing themselves from a situation they are unsure of. If we do not respect that boundary, we are more likely to get biting and growling incidents.
- Don't take advice from people who have good intentions but no idea about your dog or your training methods. Just because they rubbed their dog's nose in their mess in the 1970s doesn't mean this is a valid way to toilet-train your puppy.
- If your puppy is meeting new people, make sure that no one grabs the puppy, picks them up without them wanting it, or gets in their face. Instead have the new person sit on the floor to see if the puppy comes to them. Have lots of toys available and let the puppy lead the interactions.

- If you are having guests over who don't listen to your requests to give the puppy space, put up baby gates so your dog can be put safely behind one with chews and left alone – make it easy for yourself and your puppy.
- If your puppy is really bitey, jumpy and full on (which happens to all puppies at some stage), plan carefully when you have people coming over. Rather than letting the puppy run riot, place them in their pen and allow your visitors to sit next to the pen and push treats through or give chews. A puppy in a pen can jump up without Grandma getting injured or a toddler knocked over. Give your puppy what it needs – space to be a puppy without it impacting others and stressing you out.
- Exercise and mental stimulation are your puppy's best friends, so help your puppy be their best self by providing what they need. An exercised and mentally stimulated puppy is more likely to be relaxed around visitors.

CHAPTER TWELVE

Your Puppy in Your Home

PREVENTING BARKING

How much your puppy (and adult dog) barks will be strongly influenced by their breed, breeder and how barky their mother was. We have to set realistic expectations around barking. Most dogs bark, some are very vocal and some breeds are quieter than others. For example, a Hungarian Vizsla can be extremely vocal and chatty, and a Mini Dachshund will bark a lot.

However, there is a fine line between 'barking' and behavioural-problem barking, which is excessive and needs addressing. I cannot pinpoint a level that is 'normal' for all dogs as that greatly varies according to your breed. For example, a Shiba Inu would be very different from something like a Pomeranian's expectations for barking and yapping! If your puppy barks excessively at everything or anything, and is set off by people, dogs, kids, scooters and birds, then we would call this 'reactive' behaviour. In this case you will need to seek tailored, kind help immediately from a dog behaviourist. Don't ignore the situation, as it won't resolve itself, and please don't use YouTube, as it will create more problems than it solves. Please do not be tempted to utilise correction options such as e-collars, spraying water at your dog's face, throwing metal discs (yes, that is an actual thing that some 'trainers' do) as none of these will work and do not address the underlying issues.

Some puppies can bark in play – many collies and spaniels will do it when they are really excited or hyped up. Which isn't an issue if you are happy with it, but if you prefer to not have this, then you need to not constantly play games that hype them up and then expect them to be quiet! For example, lobbing the ball repeatedly and then your puppy starts barking because you have riled them up so much. Think about the games you play and *how* you play them, as that will help you prevent an issue rather than getting annoyed about your dog exhibiting usual dog behaviour.

We must look at dogs who I would describe as 'living on the edge' who are barking at every little sound, unable to rest and always on edge. There tends to be a medical reason for this and I would want to work with you for a deeper dive on figuring out what is going on for your dog. It shows that they certainly are not happy, they aren't feeling balanced and they are finding it very hard to regulate themselves. This isn't a fun way to live, for you or them, so please do not allow this to go on and on without seeking professional help. And never agree to work with anyone that believes in using anti-bark collars or reprimanding the dog for barking: the barking is the outlet that shows us something isn't right and it's our job to work out what that is. Not to just simply tell them to shut up.

Lastly, remember that barking can provide lots of outcomes for our puppies and dogs, so it can be useful in many ways. Barking can:

- Get your attention, e.g. a ball has rolled under the sofa.
- Make you listen when you missed all the other quieter signs, e.g. head turns, licking lips, walking away.
- Encourage another dog to interact or play.
- Get rid of another dog or keep them at bay.
- Impact the limbic system of the brain (which controls emotional drive and regulation).
- Be a result of a poor diet: with so much support needed from the food our dogs eat, if they are not getting the fatty acids, the omegas and so on, it can literally change the way the neural pathways are formed and how dogs react to stress, anxiety and more, so never underestimate the power of what you feed.
- Serve a purpose, e.g. alert-barking (there is a threat) or fear-barking (they are afraid), so understanding your dog's different barks is also really key.

WINDOW WATCHING

Many dogs love to look out of the window to see what's going on in their neighbourhood. However, some breeds or crossbreeds, like many of the Terriers and Border Collies, are extremely visually reactive and these dogs may develop obsessive watching behaviour that is very hard to remove. By obsessive, I mean a dog who sits by the window and reacts excessively to every single person, car or animal that passes, moves or goes near the house. I tend to advise clients who have big windows and a visually reactive dog to prevent this behaviour as soon as possible. The best way is to use shutters on the lower half of the windows, ensure your dog doesn't have a seat right up against the window and invest in having windows frosted so that the dog cannot see out of them but light still comes in. Otherwise you can end up with a dog who becomes obsessive around the window. This behaviour is not relaxing for you, but it also really isn't great for your dog's nervous system as they are constantly on high alert.

The fashion for bifold doors can cause problems for many dogs, as it feels to them like the outside world is in their safe space and that is incredibly hard. If you do have bifold doors, it may be worth investing in some curtains to draw (especially if you are going out and leaving the dog alone). If your dog is visually reactive, take time to think about keeping bed placement, crates and pen spaces away from big windows. And pay attention to how your dog passes their time and where they sit in the home, so that you can nip obsessive window watching in the bud early.

VISITORS WITH DOGS

If you have visitors coming over with dogs, do not simply allow them to enter the home with the dog. You will need to meet on neutral ground first, and do a walk. By neutral, I mean somewhere that is neutral for each dog. Your garden doesn't count, I'm afraid.

You will need to have set up the baby gate, so that your puppy has their own space and can be left alone if needed. All resources should be removed or be put behind the baby gate, so that squabbles can't break out.

You need to remember that your home is your puppy's safe space and only say yes to dogs you know, trust and truly feel should be in your dog's home. You should make sure there are three water bowls for two dogs, always make sure you have more options than needed, make sure food is fed separately (in different rooms or behind baby gates) and make sure there are more beds for dogs to use than there are dogs. So there should be no reason to squabble over beds. We want to set these interactions and experiences up to go well.

Make sure that the dogs have been walked properly before coming into the house, so that each dog is tired and not hyped up or going to run around like a loon. If you have a garden, you can give them access to that, so that they can potter or sunbathe in that together. However, do remember your puppy and their 'social learning' as if your friend brings their dog over and they just spend the day barking in your garden, you may end up with a puppy who begins to do the same as they are so triggered by what that dog is doing in their home.

The most common fights tend to be when multiple dogs get under the kitchen table or dining table – as you have lots of legs, food and dogs in a small space. So again, make sure dogs are separated or behind baby gates so that this doesn't occur. We still do this when my dog Pip and I, my sister and her dog, Happy, and my parents with their dog, Ted, all meet up. Ted has no aggression but can be like a bulldozer around food: he pushes past, no malice or intent, but he just sees food and goes off after it. So if that food were to land on Happy's head, he wouldn't hesitate but plough through and scoff it! Which, as you can imagine, can cause problems if you don't fancy having a sausage eaten from your head! So we manage this by Ted not being around the dining table when we are eating. If we are eating at the kitchen table, which is in the area where his bed is and where he is fed, then he is allowed in and Pip and Happy stay behind the baby gate in the hallway. There are management strategies we can put in and shouldn't apologise for, as management makes a happier home for us and our dogs.

A well-known American male dog trainer who believes in the dominance theory once stated that baby gates should not be used: a dog should be taught to stay and obey. I utterly disagree with this. Why would we not make use of a baby gate that prevents problems so that we can then focus our training time on things that build bonds, create relationships and are fun to work on. I believe in spending your time working on the things that you want and then setting your puppy up to succeed in other ways that are easy to accommodate. As life with our dogs is short, focus on the things you want to focus on, not what a bloke who believes dogs are looking to take over our world tells you!

CHAPTER THIRTEEN

Your Puppy Training

When you first bring home a puppy it can feel like you should get on board with 'training' immediately. And of course we want to make the most of those early weeks when our puppies are like little learning sponges absorbing everything – but honestly, that learning doesn't stop! I work with dogs of all ages, from tiny pups to aged seniors, and all of them share one thing in common – they will learn if it is fun.

So before you obsess over teaching your puppy to sit or stay, focus instead on building a bond, establishing eye contact, learning about your dog and understanding them. Because when you have that in place, training becomes so much easier – for both you and your puppy. When we understand our dogs, advocate for them, when we are led by them and their needs, we naturally create love. A bond and a relationship will grow from this.

A puppy that has a close bond with you will want to learn whatever you're teaching. And the first step in creating that bond is to work with your puppy on focus.

BUILDING FOCUS AROUND
DISTRACTIONS

Teaching your puppy to focus on you is not about teaching a 'look at me' cue. Instead I prefer to work with puppies and dogs and reward them when they *choose* to look at me. In my experience, rewarding something they're doing naturally sticks so much better than making them do something they don't necessarily understand or want to do. And the dog then wants to keep doing it. There are many ways we can build up our focus work, so here are a couple that work brilliantly for pups (and you can also use all of these with adult dogs too):

The bowl game: This helps your dog understand that when there are things they want or are unsure of, eye contact with you will pay off.

All you need is a bowl with some food or treats inside. Simply sit on the floor and hold the bowl up by your chest. Your dog will likely try to jump up to get at the bowl, so make sure it is out of their reach. They may then try to sit or do a 'down'. Let them. At this point they will be looking at the bowl, as they want what's inside. However, at some point they will look up at you as if to say 'come on, what are you doing?' and then you say 'yes' and reward them by placing the bowl on the ground and letting them have what's inside.

This is the simplest game ever. Within a week you can have a dog who gives eye contact immediately to let you know it wants something.

One word of warning. This is not a game to use on dogs who are always hungry, have food issues or have been starved.

The stand by the door game: To help your dog understand that they need you to help them do things.

Place your dog on a lead and stand next to a door that they want to go out of.

Simply hold the lead and make sure it has slack in it. Put your hand on the door handle and go to open it a tiny bit, so a little sliver of air and light comes in from outside. Stand and wait. As soon as your puppy looks up at you (wondering why it's taking you so long to fully open the door) you will say 'yes', open the door wide and let them go through it. We can work on their waiting at the door another time. This exercise is purely for the purpose of teaching eye contact.

What I hope you can see, in both of these games, is that they are not only quick and easy, but also based around a desire your dog already has – to get out of the door, to scoff treats from the bowl. This is called a 'functional reward'. These kinds of games are key to my training methods as they are all about teaching your puppy that in order to get what they want, they need to make eye contact with us. In other words, they must disconnect from the thing they want and reconnect with us.

And the absolute joy of building this connection is that everything else follows on from it. This is what recall is, this is what 'leave' is, this is what a 'wait' is – a dog being controlled around something they want or are interested in or scared of. So if we show them how to do eye contact, to search us out, to connect with us from day one, it becomes second nature to those dogs. Isn't that amazing?

Another way I love to do focus work is one I've already mentioned, where you make use of your front garden, your front porch or doorstep. Have your puppy on their lead next to you, watching it all. Any time they choose to look at you and make eye contact, you reward them. It's not just for puppies either. I still do this with Pip now, and he's over ten years old!

BUILDING FOCUS AROUND OTHER DOGS

Whether we live in a city or the countryside, we are always going to encounter other dogs, to varying degrees. Teaching our puppies how to deal with this and how to interact in these situations is key. If we don't teach our puppies then they cannot learn and take this into adulthood. Here are a few suggestions to get you started:

- Parallel walk and allow your puppy to see other dogs, but be rewarded with treats and play for sticking close to you.
- Don't allow your dog to go out with walkers or to a day care that allows puppies to play and wrestle all the time.
- Find dogs that love to sniff and get on with the walk for your puppy to learn from.
- Take your puppy to places with long grass so that they

can engage in using their nose and not be obsessed with what the other dog is doing.

- Don't take your puppy to meet each dog they see. Instead, use treats to teach them how to walk past the dog on the other side of the road (at a distance).
- Make sure when out and about that you are bringing the fun to walks! If other dogs give all the good stuff and you aren't partaking in the rough play, the chasing, tag and rewarding with treats, then of course your puppy is going to go and look elsewhere.

One of my clients has a rescue Lurcher who finds it very hard to disengage from other dogs, particularly while playing. When it came to walks, this client was taking their dog to a secure dog field with two friends who had dogs of a similar age and breed. When the three dogs were let off lead, they would basically bomb around the field for a full hour, not listening to their owners and running around like loons. Of course when it came time to leave and disengage the dog didn't want to.

Now I don't want to take fun out of the equation, but it is possible to keep the enjoyment and also ensure that the dog understands that it needs to listen, give attention and focus on its owner when other dogs are around. This focus is not a nice to have, it's a necessity. So here is what we agreed to work on – your circumstances will be different, but you can see how we work backwards to set the dog up to find it easier to focus and respond to its owner.

- We agreed that before meeting at the secure field, each dog would have been walked for forty-five minutes. And that pre-walk would be something that would expend energy but also mentally stimulate them, e.g. searching for treats in long grass while on a 5-metre long line, sniffy walks on the long line, playing in the river – avoiding high-arousal games like ball play or chasing games and focusing on low-arousal but stimulating output.

- When the dogs get to the field, before they interact with each other, each dog will go with its owner to a separate corner of the field. The dogs don't need to sit or lie down or obey any particular command. Instead, each owner will wait for their dog to voluntarily make eye contact with them. No bribing with treats or calling their name: the dog must choose to look. Each dog will be rewarded handsomely with a jackpot of treats when they do this. Once each dog has done this, all three dogs can be let off and told to go and play.

- Allow the dogs to have a play and (provided no dog has any resource-guarding issues) all three owners go over to where the dogs are playing and take out a very smelly treat, I find a frankfurter chunk works well. Now each owner is going to get very close to their puppy and push the treat into their dog's face. As soon as their dog reacts to the treat by turning away from the other dogs, or giving attention to its owner, it receives the treat. Each owner will be doing this with their dog, so all dogs get rewarded. If you end up with more than just your dog responding to you, that is OK, you can reward them all. Don't ask for sits, just get the treats into their mouth and keep rewarding them for ten to thirty seconds with constant

treats for choosing to stay focused on you. Then stop the treats and say 'go and play', or something similar.
- Within the one-hour walk in that secure field, the owners are going to aim to do that treat-and-attention game five times overall.
- The next week, each owner will do the same things, but before they let the dogs off lead, they will take one step forward from their corner of the field, so that over the course of several weeks in that field they get closer and closer.
- Then each week, they will build up to getting their dog's attention with their treat and then keeping their dog with them so it may be something like this:
  » Week One – treat and reward up close and personal
  » Week Two – treat and reward and take one step away and keep dog with you for thirty seconds
  » Week Three – treat and reward and take three steps away and keep dog with you for thirty seconds
  » Week Four – treat and reward and take five steps away and keep dog with you for thirty seconds
  » Week Five – treat and reward and take seven steps away and keep dog with you for forty-five seconds and so on.

The idea is to teach your puppy three things over the course of the weeks and months:

- When other dogs are around, to still check in with you and look at you when they can see them up front or in the distance.

- To listen and pay attention when asked.
- To step away from the distraction and learn that it is worth their time to do this.

Each week the owners are going to build on what they want and expect because we build it in baby steps, not giant steps that the dogs are not ready for. If we don't do these baby steps, we can't expect our puppies to understand what we want, as we haven't taught them. So instead, we work at a pace that is easy, doable and realistic – rather than setting unrealistic expectations that lead to exasperation for everyone and their dog or puppy.

SEPARATION ANXIETY AND INDEPENDENCE TRAINING

Separation distress is when a puppy starts to show fear, uncertainty or a clear reaction to being on their own. This can come in various forms. It may start simply with crying when you go for a shower and the door has been shut on them or, in its worst forms, can result in dogs who tear through sofas, doors and walls in order to try to reach their owners. It is a very real fear for some dogs and we should not downplay it. But there is so much that we can do to prevent it, to aid it and to keep our puppies feeling relaxed!

This is a huge topic that I tend to work on during tailored one-to-one sessions with clients, but in this book I can help you start to create some great habits and to really understand why your puppy may be struggling, so that we can set you on the right path to creating a happy and independent puppy.

- You must always bear in mind that your puppy does not understand where you are going if you simply shut the door on them. If you haven't taught them, why would they know – and how can you expect anything else but confusion or panic?
- Methods like repeatedly shutting the door and going back in and out are really unhelpful and can actually trigger issues in puppies that weren't there before an owner started on that kind of training. I find it doesn't help the puppy but actually makes them fixated on the trigger you have created, e.g. touching the door handle.
- The way your puppy was in the litter will impact how they deal with separation. We cannot change that, we have to work with their nature, the way they were raised and their genetics – which is why I talk about the research and the process of finding your puppy, as it impacts how you train your puppy and their behaviour such a gigantic amount.
- You do need to factor in months for separation-anxiety training as this isn't something you can do in a few weeks. All of these steps will help set your puppy up to feel confident and happy and encourage them to make their own choices, which will heavily impact their ability to not see you or not be in the same room as you – which is a major success!

How do we start our independence training?

- The first thing we do is we stop restricting the access
  our puppy has to the house. To build your puppy's
  confidence, which will mean they are happy to be
  left alone for a while, we *need* them to explore on
  their own. We need them to wander, we need them
  to go looking for trouble, things to chew, places to
  pee, things to grab – as that is independence. Please
  go back and re-read the section on puppy-proofing
  on page 72 to find out how I advise you do this.
  This giving of independence isn't up for debate,
  it isn't a 'nice to have', it is something that must
  happen from the first day you get your puppy home.
  At first of course you will block off rooms and put
  baby gates on stairs, but you must give your puppy
  freedom or else they are going to be noticing that
  you follow them from room to room, and this will
  signal to them that there may be something to be
  concerned about.
- Identify a room that your puppy favours, e.g. your
  bedroom, sitting room, front room or kitchen. It needs
  to be somewhere your puppy favours, not where you
  choose; somewhere they want to go, choose to go and
  self-select. That part is really important. Don't convince
  yourself the dog's favourite place is the utility room
  with the easy-to-clean tiled floor when actually it is
  the carpeted bedroom, as otherwise this won't work.
- In the room that your puppy has chosen, you are
  going to choose times when you know your puppy is
  tired or should be getting ready to nap. Take them

out for a toilet break, then go into that room with your puppy and make yourself inaccessible. You will be present, but you won't have contact with your puppy, e.g. you can sit on the sofa with your legs up, or on a chair at the table with your legs up, or on the bed reading. I want you to be there physically but sat on a laptop, watching TV or something else so that your attention is not on your puppy. Make sure there are objects available that calm your puppy, that they can access and chew in that room, such as a chew or a toy. Let your puppy wander around and wait for them to finally settle and snooze.

- Let them sleep while you stay where you are and carry on working/reading until they wake up. Don't be tempted to creep out, as if the puppy wakes and you aren't there it can create a situation where your pup learns to be afraid to nap as they associate it with being left and not knowing where you are.
- The next day, you will do the same thing but you will position your chair 1 metre away from where it was before and towards the door. Put your legs up and work and let the puppy find somewhere to rest.
- The next day, the same thing but another metre closer to the door and so on.
- You'll work on this until you reach the doorway, which you will have set up with a baby gate. Then you can position your chair on the other side of the baby gate, while the puppy plays and settles. Because you have spent nearly a week setting up the scene where you sitting on the chair means disengagement, the puppy has no expectation that you will play, and so

they start to associate this time with playing alone and then finding somewhere to nap.

- The next day, do the same thing to just check your puppy is OK and can settle like this. If your puppy comes to the baby gate, it is totally fine. You are there, you are present, they can see you, smell you and hear you. We are just trying to create an association that being separate from you isn't a bad thing. If your puppy starts crying, you can simply push your hand through the gate so that they can touch you, lay next to it and sniff it, but you aren't going to actively stroke them or fiddle around with them. You are just reassuring them that 'I am here, this is not scary', etc.

This baby-step system is hugely important and something I then build on with my clients, depending what stage their puppy is at. We never just shut the door on a puppy and hope for the best, and we never just walk away from them. Our dogs are creatures with emotions, designed to be with their gang. So this kind of training needs to be taken seriously but done gently.

If you are struggling with things like going for a shower and your puppy not being able to be left alone, then don't panic. Just take them with you, having puppy-proofed the surrounding rooms. Shower with the bathroom door open and let the puppy roam upstairs independently. Drop treats on the floor away from the bathroom or ask your partner to, so that puppy doesn't see the treat dropping. Leave toys for them to find while you are showering and let them have fun. When you get out of the shower and the puppy comes to greet you, just don't turn it into a big deal, say a quick hello and get on with getting ready. Don't spend time focusing on praising your puppy when they came to find you, as that is the bit they will remember because you reinforced it.

THE BASICS OF PUPPY MANNERS: SITTING, JUMPING UP AND TABLE MANNERS

A well-behaved puppy means that you are paving the way to be able to do more with your puppy. In addition, you are making your dog a brilliant ambassador for dogs. The more people who have an issue with a dog being somewhere due to bad behaviour, the more reasons they have for banning owners and our dogs from pubs, cafés, parks, buses, trains and public spaces. I really don't want our world to get smaller, so the work you put in here will really pay dividends later on, I promise!

When it comes to teaching manners to your puppy, my aim is to always start teaching these as part of daily life. Use my methods when you are playing, feeding, giving a chew, out on walks, rather than in dedicated training sessions that bear no resemblance to real life. Incorporating these 'lessons' day-to-day in different environments and with different distractions means that manners become second nature for your puppy. Let me show you what I mean . . .

Teaching a 'sit'

When you are playing with your puppy and they are in a good mood (meaning not hyped and not overtired), take a toy they are enjoying playing with. Play a little with them and the item to make sure they are engaged with it, then simply hold the toy close to your body and wrap your hands around it so that they cannot access it. I tend to do this while sitting on the floor or crouching down. They may jump up or start digging at your hands. That is fine, just ignore it. Within a few seconds your puppy will take a moment to think, which will involve putting their bottom on the ground. As soon as they do this – bingo! – give them the toy and praise them. Just do one of these each play session and you will very, very quickly have taught your puppy that when there is something they want they need to sit. It will be a marvel for you to watch them learn it on their own, and it will sink in because all you have done is capture the behaviour they were doing naturally!

Teaching your puppy to focus and listen

Your puppy's ability – and inclination – to listen to you is going to depend a lot on their breed and their breeding. So the first thing you need to consider is how ready your puppy is going to be to listen to you.

Some breeds were designed to be independent and work alone, such as seeking out rats, finding badgers, hunting without a person present or guarding sheep, like Jack

Russells, Border Terriers or Anatolian Shepherds. These dogs have been bred to make their own decisions and function independently. That is not to say that you can't teach these breeds to listen, but you have to tailor your training to their natural behaviour. In order to do this, we should look at making sure we are focusing on building eye contact, increasing focus (see the games listed on pages 283–4), and introducing play that is going to meet their desire to use their nose, jump about, grab and tug. Bringing joy to our dogs' lives will make them more dependent on us and that helps us build that relationship we so desire.

For a dog who isn't designed to take heaps of direction, we would spend our time on making sure we aren't constantly chatting to them, saying their name all the time, or telling them what to do continuously. We would not put in too many boundaries of entry – if your dog comes back to you, you ask it to sit and then reward it, this doesn't work for a dog designed to work alone. It actually works as a barrier and will demotivate them, not motivate them.

On the other hand, we may have a dog that is designed to listen to us, to be by our side on a shoot, to be an assistance dog or a human companion dog. These breeds, such as the Labrador, Golden Retriever or Cavalier King Charles, are hardwired to seek you out, to be close. They actively want direction and thrive off being given tasks. In fact, these dogs can struggle if not given enough direction. They love to learn, so it is something that deeply stimulates them and makes them happy. So for these breeds, you will find being close by and giving eye contact will be relatively easy for them and simple for you to reinforce using frequent treat supply.

Neither of these categories is better than another. But what is key is that you as an owner understand what you're working with. Because if you don't know the breed characteristics of your puppy or understand its implications for their ability to listen, it can lead to a great deal of frustration on your behalf.

If we incorporate some fun things, I promise you with all my heart that we can get your puppy to listen and to choose to listen. Here are some simple methods, applicable for all breeds of puppy, to help increase listening skills. You will notice these games don't *seem* to teach much in the way of listening and that is because, first of all we need to teach our puppy to focus and pay attention, and only then do we add a cue that they will want to listen to.

- Sit on the floor or any flat surface (not grass) with a bag or cup full of little treats. When your dog stands in front of you and looks at you, reward them by throwing a treat just in front of you on the floor and let them hoover it up. As soon as they look at you again, reward them by throwing the treat down again. Keep repeating this, but each time add in a tiny amount more distance when you throw the treat. What we are trying to establish is that your puppy starts to love the game – understanding that they look at you, you throw a treat, they eat it and dash back to look at you and you repeat. This game is so much fun to teach and dogs of both categories adore it because it incorporates movement, sniffing, attention seeking and treats.

- Hold a treat in one hand, clenching your first. Let your puppy sniff your fist, then immediately open your hand and release the treat. Do this a few more times: make it super-easy for them to understand the idea. Then after about ten repetitions of this, clench your hand closed with the treat inside, and when your puppy stares at your hand, say their name. When they either look away from your fist or look at you, reward immediately. This is teaching them to respond to you even when they are distracted.
- Identify something that your puppy wants to spend their time doing. Here are some examples to get you thinking:
  - » If your puppy loves jumping up, let's use some logs, either in the park or laid out on some grass. Call your puppy to you and when they come back, you are going to get them to jump straight up onto the log (if it's big) or over the log as their reward.
  - » If your puppy loves mouthing objects, let's use a retrieval dummy that is attached to a piece of rope/string (just search for 'retrieval dummies' online). To keep your puppy staying close to you as you walk past a distraction, you are going to say their name so they look at you. When they do, throw the dummy for the puppy to fetch while you hold the end of the rope. Let your puppy carry the dummy and mouth on it as you walk past the distraction, with you attached by the rope/string. You will remove it once past.

» If your puppy loves carrying things – let's use a 'chuck it' ball (rubber ones that have 'give' in them). You are going to use the ball to keep your dog's attention when there are distractions around by calling them back to you and immediately rewarding them with a game of catch. Not lobbing the ball a long distance, but a game where they are stood in front of you and you simply do gentle throws for them to catch the ball, release it and repeat. This is incredibly fulfilling for a dog who loves to hold things. If your puppy doesn't want to give it up, you can thread a ribbon or rope through the ball and hold onto it, while offering your puppy a treat for letting go of it.

» If your puppy loves sniffing, let's choose a toy or a treat they love. You are going to take your puppy and their chosen object to an area of long grass/bushes/undergrowth/piles of leaves. Either call your puppy to you (if they're a little way away) or say their name to get their attention. As soon as they respond by looking at you, throw the object into the grass or bushes or wherever you are for them to sniff out and find. You are teaching them that when they listen or respond they get an incredible opportunity.

» If your puppy loves running, take your long line and get ready outside. If you have a dog who is built to run or just needs to expend some energy, you are going to make yourself a part of it rather than just allowing other dogs to create all the fun for your puppy. You are going to do things like ask for your puppy's attention and then you are going to say something like 'let's ruuuuunnnn' and start jogging and let them run beside you. Then stop and say it again but change direction and keep doing this. If your puppy is a breed that may get overstimulated by running (e.g. Staffy, German Shorthaired Pointer) but does need to get rid of energy, then ensure that you do this in long grass or woodland, so that your puppy doesn't get too crazy. They will run and use their nose at the same time, so this can really help to calm that motion down. If they do, then make sure you have a tugger toy that you can redirect this onto. I'd still rather they were learning that they can play running games with you than just other dogs as it means they feel that you are part of this and that they can rely on you for fun too.

Stopping a puppy from jumping up

While most people think a little puppy jumping at their legs is cute, it's not behaviour we want to encourage as your dog gets bigger and older. To begin to work on this, I recommend dropping your reward treats on the ground, rather than giving them to the puppy directly from your hands. This means your puppy begins to learn to look to the ground rather than jumping up to meet hands and get treats. When you start using treats and rewards, I always encourage clients to reward from under the puppy's chin so your puppy gets used to looking down to get a treat rather than always upwards. It is a tiny detail but one that can transform how your puppy views taking treats and where to expect them from.

Please do note, there is a difference between a puppy jumping up to try and get a treat and one that is worried, anxious or unsure that is jumping up to get your attention to remove them from the situation. We do need to differentiate and act accordingly.

Teaching your puppy table manners

It's crucial to remember that having your dog around tables full of food is not an easy thing! But there are ways you can start to teach them how you would like them to behave from the very start.

Firstly, I would definitely recommend reading over the feeding section again, on page 193. This is important because we need to make sure our puppies are fulfilled and not needing to scavenge. Here are some ways you can start on great table manners:

- Don't feed directly from the table. Save the scraps of your food for after the meal, and give them to your puppy away from the table later.
- Lay a mat or rug under your dining table and, if your puppy is happy, you can tether them (lead and harness) to your table, so they have room to get up and turn around. On the rug or mat, you can give them a lick mat or chew to crack on with before you

sit down. If your dog has a little whine this is totally fine, they just need to get used to not having free rein around the table at your meal times.

- If table time is full-on (often the case with young kids!), use a pen or baby gate to simply keep your puppy out of the way. Management is as important as training, so try to make sure that they have plenty to do to amuse themselves their side of the gate. Even if that means leaving the door to the garden open (so long as it's safe and secure)! Let them realise table time doesn't automatically involve them.

- Another option depending on the time you have, but which will pay off in the end, is to teach your dog to voluntarily use a settle mat. Choose a comfy stable mat and throw treats onto it for them to go and eat. Wait for them to hover on the mat, and then drop more little treats on it. Then you can wait for them to volunteer a sit and reward. Give treats on the mat, not to their mouth, and build this up to your dog choosing to lay because they are a bit bored and relaxed and want more treats! Start this away from the table, like while watching TV, then slowly build it up to be while you have a cup of tea, and then to when you are making some toast, etc. Do bear in mind this takes months and isn't a 'quick fix', but it can really pay off.

The key thing is: start as you mean to go on!

CHAPTER FOURTEEN

Spaying, Neutering and Hormones

Hormones are fundamental to our dog's lives. They are pivotal to your puppy feeling happy, content, calm and at ease. Hormones also have a delicate balance that can very easily be disrupted, so reading this section is really important for all puppy owners.

Our puppies will all have varying times when their hormones start to kick in and make themselves known. We can start to see this when our puppies find it hard to concentrate, are easily distracted, want to sniff and pee on everything or rampage across fields, ears flapping in the wind, because they caught a waft of something! Rather like us, hormones can create a wild ride. They can impact how your dog eats, what they eat, how they interact with the world. They impact aggression, reactivity, sleep and so much more, so you shouldn't underestimate their power. It can often feel a bit of an uphill battle when discussing this with some vets, as many still believe that hormones don't impact a dog, but I disagree wholeheartedly and the following should show you why.

The hormones in our puppy's body are responsible for so much, which is why I never recommend having your puppy of either gender neutered or spayed before twelve months of age. Unless there is a very precise medical reason that could cause a huge impact, but that is actually very, very rare in my experience of working with dogs and puppies.

FOR OUR MALE DOGS

Male dogs' hormones give them confidence to investigate situations, to be curious and can reduce fearful interactions. So for many dogs, the longer we keep our male dog intact, the better it can serve them. As discussed in the month-by-month section on page 109, growth plates are impacted by hormones and this is just one of the things we need to consider when we operate to neuter our male dogs.

Many dogs can live happily intact for ever, but many also cannot. For some dogs, their hormones drive them to mark more, to stray more, to go off looking for bitches – so you do need to think about whether this behaviour is going to work for you and for your dog and the environment you live in. An adult male dog constantly seeking something that's not available isn't that much fun for either of you. It also isn't fair for other dog owners for your dog to be chasing, badgering and following every time you step into the park!

In an ideal scenario, I would recommend you wait until eighteen months to two years of age before neutering a dog. When we remove those hormones, it directly affects your growing dog's bone development, maturation and internal development. The earliest I would suggest neutering a male dog is twelve months (but ideally we'd wait longer), and for some bigger-breed dogs, who are slow to mature, my recommended minimum neutering age would be two years, sometimes even two and a half years to ensure their bone growth and development has matured and finished.

I would not neuter your dog early just to get them in with a certain day care or dog walker, as that would highlight to me that the walker or day care does not have your dog's best interests at heart.

In some very dog-dense areas where there are a lot of intact male dogs, often owned by less than responsible owners, your maturing male dog may experience a little too much unwanted attention from other intact male dogs. This attention may at times tip over into aggression and if you can't rely on other owners to be responsible, you have to consider your options. If your dog is at a formative age and they are still maturing but you are noticing some adult males being difficult with them, then you have three choices:

1. Neuter them earlier than planned to ensure that these interactions cease, so that your dog doesn't get bullied and in turn create reactivity issues for you and your dog due to the persistent bullying. Think really long and hard about this before you make this decision because it is a hard one to call. It would be something I would need to discuss in detail with my clients, going through the dog's full history, breeding background, temperament, where you walk and live and much more.

2. Keep your male dog intact but try to only walk them in places where your interactions with other intact

male dogs are few and far between. Instead, organise walks with happy, well-socialised males and females who can keep building up his picture of what adult dog interactions mean, i.e. calm, neutral, avoiding confrontation and scraps. This will pay off in dividends as an adult dog.

3. You can have your puppy chemically castrated – this is usually an implant that is inserted, which means that your dog keeps his testicles but ceases any hormonal production. You do need to be aware that the hormones cease and so the growth and development also stops. It isn't a miracle solution in my eyes, as the implant means you lose the benefit of the growth hormones that help with bone development. Lots of people don't realise this, but it is important to point out because it is not a wonder solution. I would tend to use this more in older dogs whose growth has stopped, but for a three- to six-month trial period to see if it helps with any behaviours. If it does, great, the op can go ahead. An example of this is a client who I only began working with when their German Shorthaired Pointer was six years old and they had not had him neutered. They were having some issues with him in the garden and in the park, and as part of our behavioural programme we looked at a trial using the implant, which you can have removed. If it helped, we could go ahead with the full operation. If there was no difference or it made it worse, we would leave him as he was. But I don't tend to use this for developing puppies.

FOR OUR FEMALE DOGS

Every female puppy will have a season, which is where the puppy starts to bleed (first seasons are often just a discharge) and this signals that the female is ready to reproduce. We cannot tell when our puppies will go through their first season as it can depend on the size of the dog, their mother, what they are fed and their own individual body clocks.

Every dog is different, so I am always loath to give 'general' advice, but in the case of female dogs I would in most situations suggest that an owner aims to spay a bitch after her second season.* (So long as the previous seasons 'went well', as in there were no complications or behavioural problems arising.)

The first season is an unknown. We have no idea when it is coming, so we just need to be on the lookout and then mark down when you think it started and when you feel it ended. What you're looking for is a swollen vulva on your bitch, and then the bleeding or discharge. You should note down when the bleeding or discharge finished and when the swelling reduced and vanished. Include also when their nipples started to swell and when they returned to normal. You can even take photos as these will be date marked. While it doesn't make for a pretty picture, it is really crucial information when we are considering when to have our bitch spayed. A season can last four to six weeks. It isn't a set amount of days. Rather like how women's cycles are each different, the same is true for our dogs.

---

* www.veterinary-practice.com/article/pseudopregnancy-in-spayed-bitches

Here are some things to bear in mind when your dog is in or coming out of their season:

- You should not be walking your dog in the park or in dog-dense areas. It can result in other dogs being distracted by your dog, who will follow them and try to keep sniffing their bottom. Some may even try to get on top of your dog and this can be really stressful. Males have been known to cross roads, run out of parks and away from their owners in order to track down bitches in season.
- Keep your dog on a long line and walk them very early in the morning and late at night.
- You may find your bitch doesn't actually want to be walked and is happy to stay at home. That is fine, don't force them out.
- Be aware that when the bleeding stops your dog will still be fertile and that is why we also keep an eye on the physical symptoms listed above, like the swelling.

All being well, our bitch will come out of her season feeling happy and back to her usual self. And then it is a waiting game for the next season, and again you are going to mark down the same events as listed for the first season. Now we need to look at what the gap was between the start and conclusion of the first season and second season, as this gives us the information we need to determine the best time to spay your bitch.

So long as you have your dates right and you have really paid attention, we would be looking to spay your bitch sixteen weeks after their second season finished – so do use your calendar and get that date booked in asap as we can't be flexible on dates. Ideally you want to find someone who can do the operation by keyhole surgery rather than opening your dog up, which takes much longer to recover from. So you might find a different vet to do the op from your usual vet, but do call around, discuss and see who you like and who you feel comfortable with.

What to do if your bitch stops eating during their season

The first thing to say is do not panic. Loss of appetite can be an indicator of a phantom pregnancy, so do keep an eye on other symptoms and your dog's behaviour. Keep a diary so you can use it to accurately discuss timings and symptoms with your vet or behaviourist (or ideally both).

Hormones can suppress or increase appetite – the same happens to women with their own cycle, so a temporary loss of appetite isn't out of the ordinary. Try not to get caught up in making sure your dog is eating an exact amount or a set portion of their food. You may need to change the time of day you feed them, or they may just need one meal in the evening during their cycle. They may have previously been eating raw but now they want cooked food. That is fine. Facilitate what they need. When they come out of the cycle and, provided they don't go into a phantom pregnancy, you should find that eating habits return to normal or you can start to transition them back over a few weeks. You may find they are more interested in chews or raw items to eat, e.g. duck necks, that will fill them up and give them nutrients. You can use bone broth to ensure nutritious intake and even serve it warm to tempt your dog.

Do just keep the possibility of phantom pregnancy at the back of your mind, as if this is the case you may need to take action (see below).

Always trust your gut instinct. You know your dog. Many vets I've had say that hormones do not impact the dog. I strongly disagree. So if you are struggling with your own vet, seek out someone who is more understanding and can assist you with what you and your dog needs. I can highly recommend Sara Davies, who is a leading vet on spaying and phantom pregnancies.

Lastly, do expect your dog to have an upset stomach, diahorrea or constipation during a season. Do not be tempted to start using gastro foods or believing that they have a sensitive stomach if what you have been feeding has worked up until now.

Phantom pregnancies

Phantom pregnancies are when a dog comes out of a season and their body believes it is pregnant or has had a litter. This time period can be incredibly distressing for you and your puppy, but it is crucial that you treat your puppy with a great deal of understanding. Going through a phantom pregnancy can impact a puppy's behaviour for ever if it isn't dealt with properly.

Here are some of the ways you may start to notice that your puppy is going through a phantom pregnancy, and the key is that their behaviour will be different to before their season:

- They start resource guarding.
- Have acute anxiety, can no longer be left or separated from their owner or family.
- Become reactive and display aggression to humans and dogs.
- Become so distressed that they destroy entire sofas trying to find somewhere to hide, which often stems from trying to create a nest for their phantom litter or to prep a nest.
- Whining and panting and unable to settle, which then exhausts them but they can't rest – this can sometimes be pain related.
- Start nesting and carrying their 'babies' around (these tend to be household objects, toys and things like socks or hairbrushes).
- Stop eating totally.
- Become lethargic, sad and do not want to leave the house.

For the dog involved, this is a period of huge impact on their personality and life. Do not underestimate it and do not try to gloss over it. I've had clients be told heart-breaking things by vets who don't understand it – they have been told to 'run the dog into the ground' so they stop nesting. Clients have been told to take away all their toys and nesting items, which causes huge distress to the puppy who is going through it. Vets have told my clients to withdraw affection and contact and leave the dog to it. All of this advice breaks my heart. Your puppy does not deserve to be treated in this way, they are suffering enough as it is.

Vets will often only diagnose a dog as having a phantom pregancy if they can see physical signs, e.g. milk coming from teats if you squeeze them, swollen nipples, swollen vulva. This isn't factually true: a dog can be having a phantom pregnancy and not exhibit those signs but show behavioural symptoms, or they can have physical and behavioural symptoms.

I cannot give general advice here because we need to know detailed information about your puppy before knowing what might help them. The vet Sara Davies has been one of the first people to investigate and learn about phantom pregnancies in our dogs, and if your dog suffers with this, I can't recommend her work highly enough. She has pioneered research, and put understanding and love into helping our female dogs.

Do just know that you can help your dog, you can get them out of a phantom pregnancy, help them recover and give them medication that stops it and reinstates their hormones to a more balanced state. This can literally remove the aggression, reactivity, fear and anxiety that came from living through a phantom pregnancy for your dog. It is crucial to find a vet who understands phantom pregnancy rather than just dismissing it, so if you feel your vet isn't that person, you are entitled to find someone else.

A Last Word on Your Dog and You . . .

There will come a day when you go out for a walk and realise that things have shifted, sunk in or feel different. This feeling isn't something you can pinpoint or name. It might happen when you realise that you are having more days and walks when things go well, or when your dog listens and looks up at you, or when you realise you don't need to call them back from yet another dog because they are sticking close to you. You realise you are entering adulthood with your puppy.

If you have chosen well and chosen right for you, and committed to your dog's development, when your dog grows up you are going to have your best friend right by your side, every day. And what an incredible honour that is, to share your life and spend time with the best creature on this planet.

I may say that a dog never stops learning, but I often say to owners not to spend so long worrying about trying to have the 'perfect' dog that you miss out on enjoying the funny, cheeky and hilarious individual that your puppy is. Every puppy is special and the way they do things will be unique to them. So don't get so caught up in your dog being so 'obedient' that you forget to enjoy who your dog is. We are never aiming for robot status, perfection or 100 per cent reliability, as that is just not possible. I have never met a human or even a computer that is 100 per cent consistent so let's not expect that of our dogs.

We sometimes lose sight of the fact that our dog is a dog! We have to build in the time for them being a dog to be encouraged and for them to feel satisfied. No one needs a regimental foot soldier of a puppy marching next to them all the time. Your puppy can be given freedom – sniffing time, permission to walk ahead or behind you. Let your dog be a dog!

I feel that one piece of advice that is missing from so many puppy books is to remember to love your dog hard! Loving and adoring your puppy does not mean letting them get away with everything. You can still have boundaries and do great training and fun things together, but make sure you lavish them with one-to-one time throughout their lives. Dedicated time with you is their biggest dream in the world. You can spend money on your puppy, but, really, the only thing they desire is your time, attention and you as a play companion. That is what builds incredible bonds.

Your puppy will love you in a way that no human has, even those humans who adore you. The love from your dog is different. There are no conditions, there is no holding back, there is no intent to cause pain or be difficult. Please remember that no dog ever sets out to do harm. Aggression in dogs is down to us as humans because of how we breed, how we socialise, how we feed, how we handle and how we train and raise our puppies.

I hope this book has shown you how to raise your puppy with understanding, love, compassion and kindness. I truly believe that if your puppy could tell you how it wants to be treated, it would tell you everything I've put into this book.

For me, dogs are the most precious beings walking this earth, gracing us with their presence, residing by our side and helping us every single day. Never forget how wonderful your dog is and, please, enjoy your time together, because it goes in a heartbeat.

L
X

Acknowledgements

I have really felt an epic responsibility when writing this book, because writing about puppies is essentially equipping owners with the skills to build a life with an incredible dog. I couldn't have devoted the time to this book without the help of so many people.

To my husband, Kyle, you have full faith in me and it means the world to be doing this with you by my side. Thank you for being so incredible.

To my children, each and every time I've had to work late or into the evening and you have moaned at me – I hope this will for ever serve as a reminder of why I was doing it, but also to always pursue and make space for the things that make you so happy. Dogs are incredible and one day you will realise you were so lucky to have so many in your life. You are both wonderful and I love you.

To my mum and dad, who I would ring after each writing session to update them on my word count! I am so happy you now have Teddy Bear to go through retirement with. He is such a dream and I truly believe that Pudding left you to make way for him to enter your and our hearts.

To Toffee, Fudge, Rosie and Daisy who belonged to my in-laws, you taught me so much and I often think about the hilarious things you used to do that informed some of my methods to this day.

To my assistant, Kate Humpherys – I am so grateful that we get to work together every day. Without you, I would be snookered.

Dr Vince McNally who I first met in 2023 when we took Ted on from the rescue. It's been a dream to find a vet who has the same views and wants to serve dogs in the same way that I do. Keep up the incredible work, you are literally transforming dogs' lives.

Pippa Wright, my editor extraordinaire who I have worked with on both books. She is a pioneer and a woman so hell bent on raising other women up. Without her, these books would not have seen the light of day. She has enabled me to transform dogs' lives and show people that there is another way. For that, we are all indebted to her foresight and love for dogs. To Beth Eynon, for being a support and so thoughtful with her input.

To Jadeen Singh, my agent at John Noel Management. She listens to my ideas, reads through everything and helps me no end, another woman I'm thrilled to have on my side.

To Jane Kellock, who once again allowed me to use her cosy London Fields office on a Sunday to buckle down and crack on with writing.

To Glynis Fenwick, my childhood childminder who sadly passed away. Glynis gave me the freedom to explore, to be in nature, to be with her collie, Sam. She was an amazing and formative part of my life.

Lastly, to every owner and their dog within my online Wonder Club – you are a joy to work with, I am thankful to get to chat to you, to see you and to answer your questions every day of the week. Having an online club for owners across the world has been a dream for me, and now it is a joyful reality. If you would like to find out more regarding my online membership club, simply visit www.louiseglazebrook.com.

Finally, thank you to Jilly Cooper, the national treasure – she has kept my mind occupied at nighttime when I need to stop overthinking things and allowed me to have escapism via her books full of horses and dogs.